TM & © 2016 Real Estate Brands Ltd. All rights reserved. No part of this work may be reproduced in any form, or by any means whatsoever, without written permission from Real Estate Brands Ltd., except in the case of brief quotations embodied in critical articles and reviews.

Real Estate Brands Ltd
PO BOX 2699
Springfield, OH 45501

For more information about Real Estate Brands Ltd please telephone 844.806.6577.

Thank You!

Thank you to everyone at ROOST Real Estate Co. that made our success possible and our clients and business partners that have stood by us through good times and bad.

A REAL ESTATE INVESTOR'S GUIDE TO PROFITABILITY

MAKING YOUR REAL ESTATE INVESTMENTS WORK FOR YOU, AND NOT THE OTHER WAY AROUND

By Chris McAllister

Founder / President / Real Estate Brands Ltd.

TABLE OF CONTENTS

Introduction	**8**
Part 1: My Story	**12**
Bankruptcy	12
Nobody told me	13
So let me tell you	13
Let me show you the money	15
The Springfield, Ohio Real Estate Crash of 2008	15
It took 10 years to hit bottom	16
We had a boom too, sort of	16
ROOST Real Estate Co.	17
Lucky Town Real Estate Co.	18
What Makes Us Different	18
Our Success after the Crash	20
My Unique Ability	21
A Personal History #1 – Blog post from January 25, 2007	23
Part 2: What Kind of Investor Are You?	
Goals, Objectives, and Attitudes	**26**
An Agonizing Reappraisal	28
Right Now in Springfield	29
My Experience as a Property Manager	29
Does Investing in Real Estate Make Sense for You?	30
'Hands On' Clients	31
'Hands Off' Clients	32
Our Most Successful Clients	33
Where to Focus	35
Buy and Hold	35
Buy and Flip	36
Buy and Sell Land Contract or Offer Seller Financing	36
Acquiring Properties	38
How I Rebuilt My Portfolio by Buying Houses via Land Contract	39
Conclusion	40
Part 3: The Landlord Advantage	**45**
Why Rent if You Can Buy?	46
Demographic Trends Favor Real Estate Investing	47
All the Cool Kids Are Investing	48
My Personal Philosophy	48
What We Believe	50
The Benefits of a Licensed Property Manager	52
An Unlicensed Property Manager Horror Story	55
The ROOST Landlord Advantage™	59
The ROOST Way™	61
Conclusion: Long Term Trends Favor Landlord/Investors	64

Part 4: Owner Profitability is Job #1 — 67

The 'Wal-Mart' Client	69
Case Study #1	71
Case Study #2	72
Stakeholders to Consider	73
The Section 8 Housing Voucher Program	73
Code Enforcement	75
The Water Department	76
Landlord Tenant Agreements with the Gas and Electric Companies	76
The State or Local Health Department	76
Be a Good Neighbor	77
Insurance	77
Property Taxes	77
Your Occupancy Rate	78
The Eviction Process	79
Late Fees	80
Repairs and Maintenance	80
Professional Management	81
Valuing a Property	81
Case Study #3	82
Case Study #4:	84
Case Study #5	86
Case Study #6	87
Case Study #7:	88
Case Study #8	89
Case Study #9	91
Cash on Cash Return	92
Avoiding Bankruptcy	93
And One More Thing – Get a Good Accountant	93
Conclusion: What Has to Happen for Housing Prices to Stabilize?	94

Part 5: Where Most People Get Hurt and Why - Repairs and Maintenance — 103

Quoting Labor and Materials	105
Our Maintenance Team	106
Maintenance Answering Service	107
What Contractors Can Expect When They Work With ROOST™	109
Top 10 Reasons to Work with ROOST Real Estate Co.	109
What We Expect From Our Contractor Partners	111
Stay Focused on the Tenant	112
Preparing a Home for a New Tenant	112
Conclusion: Contractor Overhead and the Perils of the Lowest Bid	114

Part 6: Expanding Your Portfolio — 120

2017 and Beyond	121
Investment Funds and Pool Sales	122
What to Buy and How	122

Sourcing New Properties for Purchase 123
Owner Occupants and Non-Profits VS Investors 124
Finding Out About the Best Deals First 124
Working With Your Realtor® 125
How REO Agents Get Paid 127
Purchase Offers and Negotiations 127
Multiple Offer Situations 128
Earnest Money and Proof of Funds 132
Conclusion: Low Ball vs. Reasonable Offers 132

Part 7: The Basics of Management – How We Do It   **139**
Why We Do It 140
How We Split Tasks 141
Job Descriptions 142
Marketing Our Rental Properties 148
The Application and Screening Process 150
How We Show Properties 151
Security Deposits 152
Our Application 153
The Leasing Package 156
Our Standard Lease 157
Our Lease Checklist 162
After Lease Signing 162
Collecting Rent 163
Our Management Fees 163
Our Management Agreement 163
Accounting 168
Conclusion 169

Part 8: Future Opportunities   **171**
About Brevard County – The Space Coast of Florida 173
How We Ended Up Here 174
Trends 175
Our Plans 175
Case Studies of Properties under Management 176
Vacation Property Management 183
Final Installment of My Story 183
Florida – Boom and Bust 185
About the Author 188

Appendix: Sample Business Plan   **192**
I About New Ohio Investments LLC 194
II Current Rent Roll 195
III Loan Summary 196
IV Annual Return on Investment by Property 2013 197
V Projected Return on Investment by Property 2014 198
VI Key Projects and Requested Line of Credit 199
VII Future Investments 200
VIII Financial Reports 200

INTRODUCTION

WHAT THIS BOOK IS ABOUT

I began outlining this book with a different title. I was leaning towards:

CRASH! A REAL ESTATE INVESTOR'S LAMENT-

The Boom, the Collapse, and the New Opportunities to Build Wealth In a 'Normal' Real Estate Market.

This title is not completely hateful, but it makes me sound like too much of a whiner, and I don't want to be that guy. Looking back I *did* actually have a lot to whine about, but the fact is every single person I know suffered in one way or another as a direct result of the 2008 and 2009 real estate melt-down. Some of us eventually figured out how to make the downturn work for us instead of against us.

During 2007 and early 2008 I wrote a book with my friend and business partner Brad Zitzner entitled *We Lost $1,000,000 in Real Estate in Less than Five Years and You Can Too!* The book details the myriad mistakes and successes Brad and I had investing in real estate from 2003 through 2009 in Springfield, Ohio. Unfortunately, my mistakes overwhelmed my successes, and I was forced to file bankruptcy during the worst of the real estate crash in April of 2009.

I do devote space in this book to my personal story because I believe it will be of value to many real estate investors, licensed real estate agents and brokers. In the seven years since hitting bottom, owning my story and being willing to share it has helped many of my clients get through their own struggles with short sales, foreclosures and the everyday challenges of real estate investing. My personal musings and navel gazing—including a series of blog posts I wrote in 2009—are included throughout this book under the heading "A Personal History". This diary of sorts provided a detailed insight to what was happening during the crash in real time.

I am extremely proud of how far we have come since 2009. How I managed it both as a real estate broker and as a real estate investor does make for a pretty compelling story. Therefore, the meat of this book is about what I now understand to be the fundamentals of real estate investing. I write extensively about how I, and many of my clients, have leveraged these fundamentals and built scalable and sustainable businesses in one of the toughest economies in the country. Quite frankly, if you made money in Springfield, Ohio anytime since 2009, you can make money anywhere. That is why I feel qualified to write this book and title it:

REAL ESTATE INVESTOR'S GUIDE TO PROFITABILITY

Make your Real Estate work for you and not the other way around.

The third major focus of this book is about the basics of managing real estate, and the specific strategies and tactics we employ to ensure ongoing profitability for ourselves and our clients. Throughout this book, I will be highlighting key aspects of our unique processes and methods, our team structure and the technology we use to help our investor clients succeed.

Part 1 is titled 'My Story' and provides some background about Springfield, Ohio and ROOST Real Estate Co. It sets the stage for the rest of the book. Part 2 is titled 'What Kind of Investor Are You? – Goals, Objective, and Attitudes' where I have included Traits of Our Most Successful Investor Clients. Part 3 is titled 'The Landlord Advantage'. Part 4 is titled 'Owner Profitability is Job #1'. Part 5 is titled 'Where Most People Get Hurt and Why - Repairs and Maintenance'. Part 6 is titled 'Expanding Your Portfolio'. Part 7 is titled 'The Basics of Management – How We Do It'. Finally Part 8 is titled 'Future Opportunities'.

I have also included as an appendix my business plan for New Ohio Investments LLC. This gives a template you may want to use to clarify and position your investment business in your market, and more importantly, communicate with your banking or investment partners. Feel free to read this book in any order you wish. I think each section stands on its own, so dive in wherever you like.

Chris McAllister
May 2016

MY STORY

PART 1: MY STORY

Between 2003 and 2005, I and a partner bought over $5,000,000 worth of real estate in Springfield, Ohio. It seemed like a great idea at the time. Like the rest of the country our home values were inflated by very loose and very cheap credit. We paid too much for the properties we bought and were complete novices when it came to understanding all that goes in to making investment properties cash flow. Quite frankly the only thing we were good at was borrowing money.

The houses Brad and I began buying together 2006 and 2007, and wrote about in our book, performed very well financially. However, my share of those profits fell far short of what I needed to keep my personal portfolio afloat. By August of 2008, it became clear that it was going to be impossible to turn it around. My situation was made worse when my partner, who had already relocated out of state, let me know he was in no better position to cover our monthly shortfall than I was.

During this period, investing took up about half of my time, and running my real estate offices took up the other half. It is generally understood that the crash occurred in 2008 and 2009, but the market in Springfield began to rapidly deteriorate beginning in 2006. Business continued on a downward trend through 2009 and into 2010. Since then we have had a slow and steady recovery and 2016 will be our best year since 2006.

Bankruptcy

Without a doubt, the hardest thing I ever had to live through, and the biggest, most important project of my adult life was planning, filing and recovering from Chapter 7 bankruptcy. I was embarrassed, scared and worried about what people would think. In the end however, no one cared. At the time I actually filed, and foreclosure notices for my properties started to appear in the local newspaper, everyone else was focused on their own financial problems.

Slowly, I became empowered by the idea of a second chance. I was referred to an outstanding bankruptcy attorney who happened to be an experienced and successful real estate investor. My attorney was the only person who had the skill set and background to look objectively at my situation and create a plan to come out the other side in a position to move forward and get better The process of creating the plan that led to my filing in April 2009 took over six months.

I had made a lot of mistakes and lost all of my savings during my first eight years of investing and working in real estate. What I learned in the process however was invaluable. Bankruptcy gave me the second chance I needed to go out and start being of use again. I hope others can learn from my mistakes without the downside of repeating them.

Nobody told me

No one ever sat me down and explained the potential pitfalls of real estate investing, and there is no guarantee I would have listened if they had. I didn't know a single real estate investor when I bought my first rental property. My entire education consisted of reading Robert Kiyosaki's book *Rich Dad Poor Dad* on the back porch of my house on Long Island near the end of my tenure as a District Team Leader for Target Stores in the summer of 2000.

What I took from the book was the idea that with enough OTM (Other People's Money), you could get rich buying, renting and selling real estate. The other thing I knew for sure was I did not want to work in retail anymore—what I realize now is I was just never very good at having a boss. Investing in real estate sounded pretty easy and most importantly, it was a boss-free lifestyle.

So let me tell you

In the best of times, even now from time to time, there will be dark days in your real estate investing career. Some will be really dark. Real estate investing is a business like any other. It is not nearly as glamorous as HGTV often makes it out to be. All of the endings are not happy. There is the potential to lose money and potentially a lot of money.

Being a successful real estate investor requires doing many small things right over and over again, project after project. Some people think that investing in real estate is a passive activity. That could not be further from the truth. Unless you are lucky enough to be in a commercial triple net lease situation with a national retailer, real estate investing involves active involvement of some sort or another day in and day out.

Better than average returns in any investment category are the result of the additional effort and activity undertaken to manage the asset. Sure, there are those stories about the lucky individual getting rich because he bought a certain stock at the right time, or the stars aligned perfectly, and he made a killing. But that isn't typical; active management means getting the most out of each and every asset under normal market conditions, and in doing so positioning the portfolio to fully realize maximum value should lightning strike in your favor. (Later on I will discuss where I see lightning striking right now and in the future.)

Passive stock market investing refers to buying once and holding for the long term—buy it and forget it. Active investing involves the buying and selling of individual stocks as conditions warrant and opportunities arise. Not every active investor beats the market over time, but there are many successful hedge funds out there in the world that do. There is the real possibility that day to day involvement will allow an investor to outperform the market averages.

Real estate investing and residential real estate investing in particular requires active participation on the part of the owner or their management team. The portfolios of properties we manage for ourselves and our clients generally outperform the stock market because we are deeply involved in what goes on with the portfolio day in and day out. It's not sexy by any stretch of the imagination, but it works.

Let me show you the money

Here is how I look at it. If you have a 401k worth $1,000,000, many experts will tell you that you that to preserve your capital for as long as you may live, you should not withdraw more than 4% of your savings any given year. So $1,000,000 should safely allow you to withdraw $40,000 per year, plus inflation, every year.

In Springfield, Ohio, myself and many of my clients, are earning 15% or more on single family rental housing. To earn the income equivalent of having a tidy $1,000,000 tucked away, I only need 12 to 15, $15k to $35k single family homes in my portfolio. Look for case studies of some of the properties in my Springfield, Ohio portfolio in Part 4 'The Landlord Advantage – Owner Profitability is Job #1'.

THE SPRINGFIELD, OHIO REAL ESTATE CRASH OF 2008

I think it is important to explain how I, and my real estate company, got to this point in my life and career. So allow me to establish some context and relate a bit of the history that has directly informed my life's work and this book.

The real estate downturn in Ohio was arguably not as severe as it was in hotly speculative markets like Florida, Nevada and Arizona for example. We saw our downturn begin in June of 2006. When I say 'we' I mean my real estate brokerage at the time, RE/MAX Client Choice. Our last best year was 2005. While the mix of what is selling has changed to reflect our current demographic reality, 2016 is shaping up to be a record year.

It took 10 years to hit bottom

Springfield is generally considered to be part of the Dayton, Ohio metro market, but in most respects it is its own entity. Back in the day, Springfield was a manufacturing power house. It began to deteriorate dramatically in the late 1970s and early 1980s. With the advent of globalization and the federal government's relaxed attitude toward corporate mergers and acquisitions that undermined the ownership foundation of our local economy, Springfield's economy began to decline.

I was born in Springfield in 1961 and then moved away for 20+ years to go to college and pursue a career in Corporate America. I moved back with my family in late 2000. My parents lived and worked here until they passed away. I have seen and experienced the decline of the middle class as well as the flight of the best and brightest to other areas of the country first hand. I absolutely understand the appeal of a Donald Trump and Bernie Sanders to the local electorate, because the last 30 years have not been the best of times for my hometown.

We had a boom too—sort of.

In spite of our underlying difficulties, we had our own housing 'boom' that began around 2003. Even as we continued to hemorrhage jobs and population, our local housing market was driven by the exact same thing that drove home values up across the rest of the country, easy and cheap money.

Our market was never that exciting, but clearly those of us with jobs and decent credit had no trouble moving into the houses of our dreams, and investing imprudently in hopes of getting rich quickly. Predatory lending also drove our home values up in our lower income areas. The worst of these practices continued into 2007 when the cheap and easy money backing sub-prime lending began to dry up.

The summer of 2006 was the beginning of the end. The sales numbers for my RE/MAX offices told the tale. In June 2006, our steady sales increases ceased with our first ever sales decrease to the same period the year before. Sales in June 2006 were 16% lower than sales were in June 2005.

I am sure this is a carryover from my days as a retail manager, but the one financial metric I care about in my brokerage business is how my agents are doing compared to the year before. If you are not increasing at least at the pace of the overall market, you have a problem, and that problem is going to show up on the bottom line sooner rather than later.

The next month, July 2006, our sales were up 8% to the year before. But in August, the bottom fell out with a 50% decline to the year before, and we finished 2006 23% below our 2005 numbers. Spring and summer of 2007 continued with very soft sales. Fall 2007 improved some, but we collapsed again in December 2007 and January and February 2008 were off 50% to the year before. We ended 2008 off 20% to 2007.

Finally in 2016, we seem to be returning to a certain equilibrium. Supply and demand are more balanced at all price points, and we have worked through the foreclosures that dominated the market well into 2013. As you will see throughout this book, the crash created tremendous financial opportunities for many of us, but it is impossible to deny the devastation wreaked on people's lives.

ROOST Real Estate Co.

When we first launched ROOST Real Estate Co. in Springfield, Ohio in January of 2014, people would ask me "How did you come up with the name ROOST?" I would jokingly reply that "Zillow was already taken", and to a huge degree that was true. Here is how it happened.

I had a pretty good idea of what I thought a real estate company should look like. By 2013, I had been in the business for almost 13 years. I had been an agent at a successful local firm in 2001 and 2002 and became a RE/MAX franchisee in 2003. After the downturn in 2008 I associated my team again with the same local firm and in 2012 began researching new opportunities including other franchises.

It became clear to me pretty quickly that none of the companies I met with were the right fit for me. People I trusted urged me to create my own company but the last thing I wanted was just another local 'Mom and Pop' brokerage. If I was going to do this I wanted to create a business that was both scalable and sustainable. In other words I wanted to be able to grow the business and I wanted it to succeed regardless of the inevitable ups and downs of the industry.

In early 2013 I met Andy Hayes who runs a local design firm called Hucklebuck Design. I had seen Andy's work around town and I really liked his artistic sensibility. We began a dialogue that spring that resulted in a set of brand guidelines that reflected a company I was very excited about. We defined the colors, the font, the core values of smart, passionate, supportive, approachable, and a clear understanding of where a company like ours would fit in the industry - it all fell into place!

All we needed was a name.

Now you might think that would be the easy part. It was not. Andy and I generated literally hundreds of names. At one point I even conducted an online naming contest. Every name we liked had to be run through three filters. The first was a simple Google search to see if the name was already in use. The second was to determine if the Ohio Division of Real Estate would allow us to license the name. The third was a trademark search to ensure us that name could be trademarked.

After weeks of deliberation we settled on ROOST Real Estate Co. The selection was a result of a process of elimination, but it didn't take long to really fall in love with the name. I soon got excited about the ROOST Real Estate Co. because it accurately reflects something just a little bit different in the industry and—in my opinion—is a lot of fun.

Lucky Town Real Estate Co.

Two years later, in the spring of 2015, our path to a successful trademark of the ROOST Real Estate Co. name hit a snag. I will spare you the details but suffice it to say if your name is not trademarked, you cannot sell franchises. We were up and running in Ohio and newly licensed in Florida but that did not help our legal case. So we went back through the naming process again, and to make a long story short, we came up with Lucky Town Real Estate Co.

Today, we have a trademark in place for Lucky Town Real Estate Co. and continue our efforts to secure one for ROOST Real Estate Co. We will always operate as ROOST Real Estate Co. in Ohio because we have prior rights to the name. The brand guidelines, logos, colors and so forth for the two names are interchangeable. The company through which we will sell franchises one day is called Real Estate Brands Ltd.

What Makes Us Different

One of the major differences between our brokerage and any other national franchise is that we embrace property management. The tenant and landlord relationships we have developed over the years are the foundation of our success. While property management income makes up 20% to 25% of our total sales, it directly or indirectly drives an even greater percentage of our sales income.

We have been managing property for investor clients for the past 10 years. As of this writing we look after roughly 750 units in the Springfield. We have an affiliated office in the Dayton area that manages another 700 units. In addition we have launched our property management services in the Space Coast of Florida in the Melbourne area, and are increasing our units there both in the traditional rental market as well as short-term vacation rental management.

Many of our tenants have been with us since we started managing. Existing tenants refer other tenants to us. These tenants eventually become homebuyers. Our owners become repeat buyers because they know our proven track record for success with their previous properties and know we will maximize their new investments. I will talk more about this in Part 6, 'Expanding Your Portfolio – What You Should Expect from Your Realtor/Advisor'. In the meantime, check out our two and one half minute video at www.AllAboutROOST.com for more about how our brokerage integrates sales and management.

Our Success after the Crash

When I first got my real estate license in 2001, I had never been in business for myself and had never worked on commission. I was driven to replace the steady income I had been earning in my corporate job. My approach to selling real estate was like being shot out of a cannon. I ran down every lead and followed through on every opportunity that came my way.

One of these opportunities was listing foreclosed properties for banks and financial institutions. These are referred to as Real Estate Owned by the banks that own them or as REO's. REO listings were coming to me because none of the other real estate agents wanted them.

They did not want them because they were generally low value homes in very poor condition. The commissions earned on these sales were generally $1000 or less before the agent's split with the brokerage. For a successful agent, they were a waste of time compared to a 'retail' listing for a past client or referral.

These listings were complicated too. There are strict rules and procedures that must be followed, weekly inspections and broker price opinions that have to be completed. Property preservation tasks must be performed and often paid for out of the agent's or broker's pocket. The agent must then go through sometimes absurd reimbursement procedures to pay themselves or their broker back. For most agents, this was not worth the $500 or so they ultimately collected after their commission split.

These listings often involved helping the current occupants of the properties, sometimes tenants, sometimes former owners, secure 'Cash for Keys' from the bank. Often it was less expensive and easier for the bank to offer cash to the occupants to help them move out and secure a new place than it was to go through the eviction process.

I did not care how hard these listings were. I took every one I could get and I am very thankful I did. The relationships I established with the asset managers responsible for these properties led to more and more work for more and more different banks. Just as importantly these relationships and resulting listings led to tremendous opportunities for me and my clients to make a lot of money after the crash.

The REO business in 2011 and 2012 was almost 40% of our business. It peaked in 2013. At one point we were closing up to 30 transactions a month. For five years straight we were recognized as one of the top five real estate teams for transaction sides by the Ohio Association of Realtors. I will talk more about how the REO business works in Part 6, 'Expanding Your Portfolio.'

My Unique Ability

After 16 years in the business I am pretty clear on what I am good at and what I am not. My goal as an entrepreneur is to spend as much time as possible focused on the one or two things I am better at than anyone else. I do my best to build a team around me that compliments my strengths and allows all of us to do what we do best.

The property management services we provide allow our owners to do what they do best as well. Whether they are full time investors or investors who have full time jobs in other industries, my goal is take any distractions I can off their plates.

My unique ability is creating business opportunities and strategies designed to support and add value to the lives of real estate professionals and their clients. I love working with my clients and the sales agents in my offices and seeing them succeed. I look forward to working closely with our future franchise owners and partners bringing the ROOST/Lucky Town brand to new markets.

Never once during the darkest days of 2008 and 2009 did I consider getting out of the business or not working for myself. I do not love to work under pressure with 'my back against the wall.' However, the fear of ever having to punch a clock or work for someone else again drove me to figure this business out. Bankruptcy gave me a chance to start over, and I was determined to make the best of it.

A PERSONAL HISTORY #1 BLOG POST FROM JANUARY 25, 2007.

A Speculator's Lament

As I write this it occurs to me that it is easy to come off as being completely down on real estate as a career and investment vehicle, given current market conditions. I can assure you that this is not the case. At **My Real Estate Life***, our goal is to share what is, and has worked for us, as well as what has not. This is the central theme of our upcoming book **How I Lost a Million Dollars in Real Estate In Less Than Five Years – And You Can Too!** (Who can resist picking up a book with a title like that?)

In 2002 I partnered with a local loan officer and began purchasing property in the Clark and Champaign Counties of Ohio. We had just opened a new RE/MAX office which I was managing and all was right with the world. My partner was responsible for sourcing deals and securing financing. I took care of purchasing details, monthly management and tenant relations. We purchased over 75 units in 12 months and soon hired a property manager.

During this time it was easy to secure financing at very attractive rates. Even though we were paying top dollar for properties, values were slowly trending up and we believed the attractive financing would allow us to cash flow. In addition we felt very clever in that we supplemented our required out of pocket down payments – generally no more than 15% to 20% - with commission dollars earned from representing ourselves in the transactions. We still had to bring the full down payments to the closing table, but the next day we paid ourselves back through the commissions passed through the real estate brokerage.

*My Real Estate Life was an idea Brad Zitzner and I had to package what we had put in our book as a training program for real estate investors. We did not get very far.

Our strategy in a nutshell – borrow as much cheap and easy money as we could and put as little cash into the deal as possible. Oh yes, and then get rich!

Our first sign of trouble came with the property tax bills. We failed to anticipate what happens to commercial property assessments when properties last sold many years ago for far less than we paid for them. In some cases our property taxes went up over 50% overnight. In addition, basic monthly maintenance and repairs were far more than we budgeted for and our vacancy percentage was twice our plan.

Within a couple of years, it was clear that our cash flow schemes were doomed. I don't mean doomed that there was no positive cash flow but that we were in a negative cash flow situation. What we thought would let us each several hundred dollars a month and a nice depreciation deduction on our taxes, turned in to costing us several thousand dollars a month and no tax problems at all to worry about.

Our strategy would have worked out had our property values continued to appreciate and our economy simply stabilized instead of declining. Our favorable loan terms also began to evaporate this year as several of our commercial loans were set to adjust upward. We now know that we never really stood a chance with the limited amount of equity we had in the properties. We were, and still are highly leveraged across multiple properties. If we were in the 60% to maybe 70% loan to value range across fewer properties, we would have a lot more flexibility right now and would be closer to breaking even.

Things really began to look bleak in late 2007 and early 2008. It was getting tougher and tougher to meet monthly expenses and another tax bill was looming. Fortunately, two of our three largest apartment complexes on which financing was about to adjust and we had seller second mortgages on, went under contract at the end of the year. Both properties closed in January 2008. Though we lost a significant amount of money, we were able to harvest enough cash to buy us 12 months of time without any personal subsidies. We are now sprucing up and listing the rest of our properties for sale.

The rental market is finally firming up to some degree as many who could have gotten a subprime loan in the past cannot today. These people will remain in the rental market for some time. We have very little pricing power however. Our ability to raise rents in the face of rising taxes, insurance, maintenance and utilities is virtually nonexistent.

Still, we persevere and we may still come out ahead in the long run. The long run will continue to mean a monthly loss for the foreseeable future. Therefore, to sell now, even at a loss, is preferable to holding on. In a declining market, cash is indeed king.

Obviously we would not be here today if we had not learned from our mistakes and found other real estate ventures that have paid off handsomely and continue to. I want to believe that I have learned some important lessons through this experience that will stay with me for the rest of my life. Mainly, even in real estate, you cannot borrow your way to wealth. Live and learn.

WHAT KIND OF INVESTOR ARE YOU?

PART 2: WHAT KIND OF INVESTOR ARE YOU?- GOALS, OBJECTIVES, AND ATTITUDES

My real estate investment plan is simple: I buy for cash flow as a rule and any appreciation I realize is a bonus. My goal is to be able to make money in any market. I will actively position myself for a profitable sale should the opportunity arise. However, that sales price has to be exceptional to give up the cash I have come to enjoy. I look at the cash flow from my rental portfolio as an annuity, that when properly managed, will support me for the rest of my life. Cash flow is king.

Short term gains are nice, but they are often temporary. The reality is that the market that allows the profitable sale is also the market that may preclude you from buying new properties to replace that cash flow. In other words, you may find yourself with cash on hand with nowhere to invest it that makes sense. So, unless you have debt to pay off or think you can time the next downturn and drop in values to make a better buy, think long and hard about that short term gain relative to the long term annuity.

Real estate without debt is the most amazing cash flow machine in the world. Debt is what cripples and bankrupts so many real estate investors. Debt has its place and I use it, but I will only finance a property to term. This means I will not take out a loan with a 20 year amortization and a 10 year balloon payment. There is no guarantee that financing will be available at rates that make sense in 10 years. The only way I would do this is if I knew I could pay off the loan in 10 years.

So in a nutshell, I buy and hold. I do not flip properties. Cash flow is king. Debt is death. Real estate markets change every few years. Access to financing can change even faster based on world events that have no bearing on the local market. And finally, I think investors make more mistakes in markets that are doing well than they do in markets that are struggling.

I may be wrong but I cannot imagine that my mortgage free properties will ever not be profitable. I like that feeling of security. Having said that, let me share this front page story from The Financial Times, May 11, 2016.

Middle Class Takes Financial Hit in Most US Cities This Century by Sam Fleming and Shawn Donnan in Washington

The drivers of the middle-class squeeze vary from city to city, but some of the steepest income declines were seen in cities hit by industrial job losses in recent decades. Springfield, Ohio, saw incomes fall 27 per cent over the period, while the Detroit-Warren-Dearborn area of Michigan recorded an 18 per cent drop in incomes. Nationwide the number of manufacturing jobs shrank 29 per cent during the current century.*

* http://www.ft.com/intl/cms/s/0/695bfa18-1797-11e6-b197-a4af20d5575e.html#axzz4Ao9mPxFN

Yes Sir, that's my hometown that leads the decline.

An Agonizing Reappraisal

In 2008 and 2009 our local market—along with much of the country—was in free-fall. It was impossible to turn to any mass media outlet and not be deluged with bad news. Many long-time banking and real estate professionals identified the downturn as the worst since the Great Depression.

Since 2008, the mortgage industry has worked its way through a gut-wrenching but necessary transition. Easy money is gone, 'Liar Loans' have disappeared, and the vast majority of people need to at least bring some money to the closing table to buy property. However, I have seen some things in the lending industry of late that lead me to believe the lessons learned just seven years ago are starting to fade.

I have seen stories of major banks offering conventional loans with three percent or even lower required down payments. I saw a local real estate deal on an apartment complex where the out of town buyer borrowed money from a credit union in Illinois. I recently visited Nashville, Tennessee and was awestruck by the sheer number of residential high rise construction projects that were underway. I do not see how, even with the large numbers moving south, this influx of inventory cannot negatively impact current property values.

You can see the same kind of condo building frenzy in Miami, Florida. Which is just crazy after what Florida went through over the last few years. Anecdotal evidence? Yes. But to me, this means we need to be alert to the next big buying opportunity. Savvy real estate investors with cash used the last downturn as a once in a lifetime buying opportunity. I hope to be able to do the same during the next downturn.

Right Now in Springfield

Our market now in 2016 is better balanced, though in some neighborhoods and at certain price points, there is a shortage of inventory driving prices up at least for now. Lending levels are returning to normal. And for now at least, we seem to be enjoying reasonable levels of appreciation. Appreciation comes in cycles however, and interest rates do not stay artificially low forever. It is getting harder and harder for me to find deals that make sense, but I now know from experience, this too is temporary.

My Experience a Property Manager

I first assembled a team to manage properties for myself and my partner in 2003. That team started with me but soon grew to a bookkeeper and then a full time maintenance person. We used QuickBooks for our accounting software. As we acquired more and more rental units we soon began to stumble. The main reason was we did not anticipate all of our expenses and we were overly optimistic about our ability to raise rents. In short, it was a disaster. As a wise man once said, "if you are not earning you're learning." I sure was not 'earning' and thankfully, I learned a lot.

The inventory we were managing steadily declined as we lost properties to bankruptcy and foreclosure. However, thanks to the purchase and sales activity Brad and I were doing in 2007 and 2008, we were able to hire a licensed agent to help us buy and sell and look after our rental units. We carried on blindly for some time but slowly developed the skill sets and the processes that allowed us to get our arms around the business of management.

It was around this time that we acquired our first property management client. A past client and business partner of mine had 20 units that he and his wife were managing and it was taking too much of their time. It was also taking time away from their primary business and means of income. They wanted to continue be involved, especially with repairs and maintenance, but they wanted someone else to take over the day to day and accounting and tenant relations functions.

By this time my wife Kelly was working full time for the brokerage in accounting and bookkeeping. She also kept the books for our rentals and for our growing group of landlord clients. In March of 2009 our daughter Gretchen joined us as a licensed sales agent and within a few short months became our first full time property manager. Our staff continued to expand as more and more owners came to us for help. Buy 2010, I was actively pursuing new property management clients and by 2014 we were looking after almost 600 rental units. We manage 750+ units today.

Does Investing in Real Estate Make Sense for You?

If you are already in the business, you can skip this section. If you are just getting started or thinking about investing in real estate, you may find this useful. First of all, regardless of what so many of the best-selling real estate investing authors write, real estate is not for everyone. If you are looking for a way to get rich quick, real estate is not for you. However, if you want to supplement your income over time, or diversify your investment portfolio, and potentially enjoy some tax benefits along the way, real estate can be pretty amazing.

This may sound obvious, but you must understand that real estate is not a liquid investment. You cannot go in and out of the market easily at a moment's notice. Successful real investing requires time to pass to reach its full potential. Whether time has to pass in order to earn some appreciation, or to pay off debt, or to wait for the market to catch up to your ambition, success in real estate takes time.

Most importantly, what if the investment does not work out? Are you financially able to absorb a loss, or in a worst case situation, months of negative cash flow? Can you withstand the emotional roller coaster of a less than perfect property, transaction, or tenant? This business has more than its share of ups and downs. If you don't think you can weather a storm or two, real estate investing may not be right for you at this time. Maybe later.

'Hands On' Clients

A few of our clients are involved with the maintenance and upkeep of their properties. These clients usually see themselves as full time investors, or their primary business is home construction, maintenance, or remodeling. Generally, what these clients bring to the table is a team, or personal expertise, in general contracting that saves them significant money when rehabbing a new purchase or upgrading a property between tenants.

I consider these investors 'Hands On' clients in the very best sense. They are experts at the construction site of the business. In our experience these relationships are great because repairs and rehabbing are where most investors lose significant amounts of money. This will be made clear in Part 5 of this book Repairs and Maintenance – Where Investors Get Hurt and Why.

I am not an expert in construction, but I know what to look for. I try not to tell a skilled tradespeople how to do their jobs. I have never had the urge or desire to step in and work on a property. I am far better at other ways of making a living. I don't have the skills and I have no desire to acquire them. But if I was an expert, there is no questions I could save money doing at least some of the work myself.

'Hands Off' Clients

The vast majority of our clients have full time jobs in other industries. They are accountants, doctors, lawyers, small business owners, and executives in large corporations. They have made their money elsewhere and are looking to make more in a diversified manner that does not require additional personal effort. They are using their money, and in some cases their banker's money, to make more money.

The remainder of our clients are made up of what I call 'Accidental Landlords'. These are owners who generally only have a single house that they acquired from a family member, in an estate, or maybe elected to rent their home out after buying a new home. They almost always fall under the category of the 'Hands Off' investor.

Our Most Successful Clients

I have worked with hundreds of investors at this point in my career. Over time I have compiled a list of personal traits of successful investors. These include:

- They are all excited to talk about their business.
- Willing to learn
- Coachable
- Financially stable
- They can't wait to hear the details of a great deal.
- They act quickly and decisively if the numbers are right.
- They try to obtain as much information about a deal as they can, as quickly as they can, over the telephone.
- They trust our opinion as investors and Realtors®
- They read books and travel to seminars all around the country.
- They seek out advice from many successful people
- They understand their personal strengths and talents
- They surround themselves with a gifted core group of people.
- They consciously do everything they can to focus on the one or two things they do best and that make them the most money.
- They are open to learn and willing to try new things.
- They see themselves as entrepreneurs and business owners.

- They set goals and drive for results.
- They work well with all sorts of people.
- These people all possess a 'Play to Win' attitude.

In contrast, less successful investors seem to have these traits in common:

- These people are generally not excited to talk to us.
- They seem to be suspicious and at times even combative.
- They tend to dwell on opportunities for prolonged periods of time before making a decision.
- They want to see the property before asking any questions about the financials.
- They are skeptical of us and view us as 'sales people' versus qualified professional real estate consultants.
- If they attend seminars at all they are always local and always with the same group of people.
- They seem to only take advice from the same people over and over.
- They want to do everything themselves
- They struggle with building a team
- They are afraid to develop the talents or capabilities they need to be successful.
- In general, we see these people as 'playing not to lose'.

Looking back over my career there were several times where had I waited a bit longer to consider all of the ramifications of a purchase, I might have talked myself out of it. Sometimes that would have saved me money and heart ache but more often than not, hesitation and the loss of an opportunity would have been more costly.

The last thing you want to do as an investor is let 'analysis paralysis' set in. There is a certain amount of risk in every investment but it is the risk that creates the reward. I want my investor clients to be armed with all of the information they need to make well informed decisions and manage their risk.

Where to Focus

There are a multitude of ways to make money in real estate. Here are the three most common that I and my clients are the most familiar with.

- Buy, Fix, Rent, and Hold – Usually segmented by market.
- Buy, Fix, and Flip – Usually for short term gain.
- Buy, Fix and Sell via Land Contract or Owner Financing – A hybrid of the first two approaches.

Buy and Hold

When I started buying rental properties I really did not have a strategy beyond purchasing what I considered middle-market properties that commanded average to above average rents at the time. My goal was to buy in established working class neighborhoods. I was not looking to buy and rent low-end properties nor was I looking to buy and rent high-end properties. I was able to finance my first few properties with 20% down at a local bank as these properties were in good condition at the time of purchase.

Later, when my first partner and I started buying together, we had even less of strategy beyond buying everything we could with bank financing and as little of our own money as possible. As you already know this strategy ended badly, but I digress.

Buy and Flip

When Brad and I first started investing together there was a sweet spot where we could buy foreclosed properties on the open market inexpensively. We would then have them repaired to the standard suitable for FHA or VA financing, and then list and sell them through my brokerage.

Our strategy here was to buy anything that we thought would yield us a profit of at least $20,000. This worked for quite a while and may be a viable strategy where you are today. When the market changed and we could no longer easily sell our houses outright, we began offering our houses for rent.

Buy and Sell Land Contract or Offer Seller Financing

Buying a home, rehabbing it if necessary and then selling it to a willing and able buyer via land contract or seller financing is a fantastic strategy in an appreciating market. Selling houses via land contract makes far less sense in a stable market or an economic environment where property values are falling.

HERE ARE THE WIKIPEDIA DEFINITIONS OF

Seller Financing
(https://en.wikipedia.org/wiki/Seller_financing)

and Land Contract
(https://en.wikipedia.org/wiki/Land_contract).

Seller financing is a *loan* provided by the *seller* of a *property* or *business* to the *purchaser*. When used in the context of residential real estate, it is also called **"bond-for-title"** or **"owner financing."**[1] Usually, the purchaser will make some sort of *down pay-*

ment to the seller, and then make installment payments (usually on a monthly basis) over a specified time, at an agreed-upon interest rate, until the loan is fully repaid. In layman's terms, this is when the seller in a *transaction* offers the buyer a loan rather than the buyer obtaining one from a *bank*. To a seller, this is an *investment* in which the return is *guaranteed* only by the buyer's credit-worthiness or ability and motivation to pay the *mortgage*. For a buyer it is often beneficial, because he/she may not be able to obtain a loan from a bank. In general, the loan is secured by the property being sold. In the event that the buyer *defaults*, the property is repossessed or *foreclosed* on exactly as it would be by a bank.

A **'land contract'** (sometimes known as a **"contract for deed," "agreement for deed," "land installment contract"** or an **"installment sale agreement"**) is a contract between a seller and buyer of *real property* in which the seller provides *financing* to buyer to purchase the property for an agreed-upon purchase price and the buyer repays the *loan* in *installments*. Under a land contract, the seller retains the legal *title* to the property, while permitting the buyer to take possession of it for most purposes other than legal ownership. The sale price is typically paid in periodic installments, often with a *balloon payment* at the end to make the time length of payments shorter than a corresponding fully *amortized* loan without a final balloon payment. When the full purchase price has been paid including any *interest*, the seller is obligated to *convey* legal title to the property to the buyer. An initial *down payment* from the buyer to the seller is usually also required by a land contract. The legal status of land contracts varies from region to region.

Seller financing or land contract deals are often structured to term meaning the seller will carry the note for the life of the loan. More often than not there is a balloon payment involved at the end of a given period, usually two to five years. At the end of the term the buyer will presumably obtain a traditional mortgage and 'cash' the seller out. In an appreciating market the likelihood of a successful cash out to the investor is very high. In a stable or depreciating there is the chance that the property will not appraise at the agreed upon price and the sale will fall apart or at best be restructured.

The advantage of selling houses this way in an appreciating market is primarily because all parties stand a great chance of coming out ahead on the deal. The investor is able to sell the home at an anticipated two or three year value based on the current appreciation trend. The buyer is able to get into a new home today even though he may not be credit worthy in the eyes of a mortgage broker.

A great deal is structured so that everybody benefits from market appreciation. A smart investor will structure a deal so that there is a good chance the buyer's ultimate cash out price at the end of the term is somewhat below market. When that happens, everybody involved wins.

At the end of this book I have included a short business plan for investors interested in buying, rehabbing and selling houses via land contract in Melbourne and Palm Bay, Florida. The population of the Space Coast area of Florida is exploding mainly due to the growth of the aerospace industry. Values are steadily increasing and many new arrivals need a seller financing opportunity because they are two or three years away from qualifying for a mortgage on their own.

Acquiring Properties

There are many books, seminars, and home study courses written by industry 'gurus' that teach how to buy houses with little or no money down. I question the ethics of most of these purveyors of get rich quick schemes. These tactics have no place in this book. I hope I have not disappointed you.

Buying real estate takes at least some cash, either your own, a partner's, or a bank's. Accessing bank financing is as hard as it has ever been and generally requires a significant amount of money down. Furthermore, the condition of the investment property generally has to be fairly good. At a minimum, it must have heat, running water, and electricity. This eliminates many foreclosure opportunities from consideration. I will discuss financing in some detail in Part 6, Expanding Your Portfolio,

Including the establishment and use of lines of credit to purchase investment properties.

For now let me just state what may or may not be obvious. It is possible to buy property in a place like Springfield, Ohio, for very little money. However, the condition of the property will be poor and will require a tremendous of amount of physical effort on your part to put it in service, or a significant amount of money to pay someone else to put it in service.

So one way or another, a low to average price house in the City of Springfield is going to cost $25,000 to $30,000. You may be able to acquire a property for as little as $2500, which I have done, and put $20,000 to $25,000 in it to put get it in service. On the other hand you may buy a property in move-in condition for $25,000 to $30,000. Either approach is going to yield a property in your portfolio that will rent for $550 to $600 a month.

The first approach requires a lot less money up front and usually a huge investment of sweat equity. It also allows you to improve the property as you have cash available, either from other rental properties in your portfolio or your full time job. The second approach is probably preferable if you have the cash up front, or bank financing. The interest and principle required to service bank debt is going to impact your profit to some degree and your cash flow to a substantial degree. We will delve deeper in to this in Part 4, The Landlord Advantage – Owner Profitability is Job #1.

How I Rebuilt My Portfolio by Buying Houses via Land Contract

Within a just a couple of years after the crash and my subsequent bankruptcy I was anxious to get back into investing. I was not interested in borrowing money however. Unencumbered real estate – real estate without debt or mortgage – is a very beautiful thing. My goal was to acquire as much as I could afford.

An investor client of mine was in the habit of buying multiple properties at sheriff sale and tax sales at rock bottom values. These properties were in very bad shape. They were literally uninhabitable most of the time. My investor friend would then sell them to me via land contract at a substantial markup. I would then fix them up using the cash flow I earned from my brokerage business and with help from the people and resources we put in place growing our property management department.

The purchase price of these properties ranged from $2500 to $10,000. As a rule I would make an interest only payment for six to 12 months while I put the property back in service with my cash and effort. After the initial six to twelve month period we would term out the loan usually over 30 to 36 months. My investor client was very happy and I managed to accumulate over a dozen cash flowing properties free and clear within five years. I continue to work with this investor to this day and it has been very profitable for both of us.

Conclusion

We have covered a lot of different topics in this chapter. The key take away to me is taking the time to not only assess your market to identify the best opportunities, but assessing your personal goals, objectives, attitudes and motivations. There is no right or wrong way to invest in real estate, but your approach must be situational. Your plan has to make sense where you are. Most importantly, you have to have a plan. Your plan may/probably will change, but you have to start somewhere.

PEAK LIFESTYLE AND OUR HABIT OF ASSENT - FEBRUARY 2009

The February 2009 issue of Esquire Magazine featured an article by Tom Junod entitled "What the Hell Just Happened?" In the article Junod writes about the cultural, political, and ultimate economic impact of September 11, 2001, and the profound change the country is currently experiencing as we head into the Obama era.

Junod makes two assertions that I think relate directly to real estate investing as we assess the opportunities resulting from the collapse of the housing market. The first assertion, our 'habit of assent' provides insight into how the bubble came to be in the first place, and the second, the idea of 'Peak Lifestyle' speaks to our future as economic creatures of consumption.

We pride ourselves at My Real Estate Life for sharing the truth about our successes and failures and encourage our community to do the same so that others may learn. Brad and I describe our new book, How we Lost $1,000,000 in Real Estate in Less Than Five Years – And You Can Too (now available on Amazon.com) as being 'beyond the infomercials, beyond the hype, real estate investing in the real world'. The truth of our current situation matters because the 'get rich quick' hype of the last seven to eight years has resulted in enormous cost to hundreds of thousands of individuals and the country as a whole.

Junod believes that we are in the habit of agreeing, concurring with, or subscribing to just about anything that comes our way. We agree to specific terms and conditions of service for every product we buy, download, borrow, use, view, read and consume. We assent to authority, popular opinion, well executed marketing strategies, and literally hundreds of other small demands everyday with no critical thinking on our part.

It's just easier that way.

How else do we explain how otherwise well educated, rational consumers and investors found themselves falling forward into a banking, mortgage industry, and housing bubble and subsequent meltdown? How do we explain Bernie Madoff's Ponzi scheme? Why did so many of us assume, without investigation, that housing values would continue to appreciate because they always have? (They have not.) Why did so many of us buy into the notion that a no-income verification mortgage was a good thing? Why did we decide that home ownership was a good thing for every single citizen? Ownership entails certain responsibility; it is not for everyone and never will be. When did we all agree that free lunches were real and fiscal responsibility was an antiquated notion?

I apologize for sounding like a cranky old man but things have got to change and they are changing. Real estate investing is not for everyone. It is work, it costs money, and there is risk. It can be incredibly rewarding financially but it is not easy. You cannot borrow your way to riches and the idea of 'passive income' is just another lie we have agreed to without question. Even real estate owned free and clear takes an active interest and mental effort to manage, maintain and trade.

Question the so called experts, use your common sense, if something seems too good to be true, don't walk away, but be skeptical. Investigate. Learn to perform due diligence.

Peak Lifestyle

Theorists have been writing about Peak Oil, Peak Water, and Peak Food for a while now. The idea is that most of our natural resources are finite and at some point we will pass the half way point in terms of depletion. Our Peak Lifestyle, or the point where our 20th century capacity for consumption reached its apex may very well have occurred sometime between 2005 and 2007. Never before in history have we borrowed so much, spent so much, or consumed so much. And on what did we spend it? Bigger houses, faster cars, and 'bling'. We invested next to nothing in our future as individuals, families, or as a society.

Clearly our excesses of the past have caught up with us. Just as banks are struggling to strengthen their balance sheets, so are families and individuals. 'Bling' and excess are becoming politically incorrect as the humble Honda surpasses the Hummer H2 in the status wars. This retrenchment is painful and nowhere more so than in housing. And while I am grateful that our collective past behavior is making historic opportunities available to real estate investors who kept their heads during the boom times, the transition is stressful as we are all still in uncharted territory.

There is no shame in buying a house one can afford. Having some skin in the game when purchasing a home is a good thing. A 3.5% FHA down payment requirement, or a 5% to 10% conventional down payment requirement is enough to ensure a feeling of personal investment, and more importantly, screen out buyers who should rent. It is only since the early 2000's that these requirements vanished from the real estate scene.

It is the same argument for investors. How many properties cash flow positive after interest, taxes, insurance, maintenance, repairs, vacancies and management fees with an LTV of even 80%? Buying an investment property with 20% down was considered to be a conservative purchase during the boom times. I think many investors are realizing they would be a lot more comfortable right now if they had bought half the properties they did with twice the down payment on each.

Our new financial conservatism will be a good thing for all of us in the long run. And hopefully, the process will remind us again of what is really important to each of us in life. We at My Real Estate Life want to hear your thoughts and stories. Join our community of investors at *www.MyRealEstateLifeOnline.com* .

THE LANDLORD ADVANTAGE

PART 3: THE LANDLORD ADVANTAGE

I have said it already and will repeat it again. It is an incredible time to invest in residential real estate. Being a landlord has never been more lucrative, and with the right tools and team around you, it has never been easier to succeed. Demographics, societal norms, individual expectations, and just plain necessity have come together to create tremendous opportunity.

There are 82 million people in the United States born between the early 1980's and the early 2000's. This cohort is known as the 'Millennials' or 'Echo Boomers'. The Baby Boomers, the last great demographic wave that changed the world, totaled roughly 77 million people. The financial crises of 2007 and the resulting housing crash in 2008 and 2009, set this demographic wave back a good five to ten years. The fact of the matter is that sooner or later, and I believe sooner, these people will want a place of their own.

Since 2007 the number of young people between the ages of 15 and 34 living at home has grown dramatically. In addition the number of unmarried couples has grown and the birthrate has dropped. These trends will not last as the economy continues to expand. The inevitable outcome over the next few years is that household formation will explode. I believe many of these family will choose to rent.

Why Rent if You Can Buy?

People choose to rent for a number of reasons. Sometimes they rent out of necessity. Often they do not have the financial stability, credit history, or sustained and documented income necessary to qualify for a mortgage. For many people their status as tenants is temporary. We are still seeing people who lost their homes during the crash continue to rent but who are positioning themselves to buy in the near future. Some of these people are great candidates for land contract or seller financing purchases.

In my experience the biggest factor limiting first time buyers is student loan debt. I have strong feelings about this. Thousands of young people, and some older people who lost their jobs during the recession, are saddled with student loan debt they will never be able to repay. Even those who managed to obtain a degree are unlikely to get a job that pays enough to justify the cost. Student loan debt is protected debt that cannot be discharged in bankruptcy. It will follow many of these students their entire lives. Many of these people will always be tenants.

On the other hand, many people simply do not want the responsibility of home ownership and are happy to pay a premium for housing if they do not have to be responsible for long term upkeep and care. It is easier and more affordable to rent in an urban environment versus buying as well. The aspiration to live in a city for many young people overrides the desire to own. Some 'Empty Nester's prefer the freedom to be able to travel on their schedule and terms. Being tied to a home limits personal freedom for some people.

Demographic Trends Favor Real Estate Investing

The great recession changed what people think of as the American Dream. The last few years have been a nightmare for many home owners. The loss of equity, being upside down on the mortgage, and the need for mobility – i.e. being able to go where the work is – has for many people stricken homeownership from their list of lifetime goals. We are seeing continued population declines in rust belt states and increases in the south including Florida. I am going to write a lot more about Florida at the end of this book.

According to the U.S. Census Bureau, the seasonally adjusted national homeownership rate stood at 65.3 percent in the fourth quarter of 2012. That was a big dip compared with the peak of 69.4 percent in 2004 but comparable to the 65.4 percent rate at the beginning of 1996. (http://www.bankrate.com/finance/real-estate/nation-of-renters.aspx)

Obviously more and more people are choosing to rent their

homes than buy. 34.6% of the population require a home to rent. Many of these people will rent their entire lives. Some will only rent as necessary. Some will eventually buy – and some of these will sell and rent again. Attitudes toward renting vs. home ownership have, and are changing rapidly for more than a third of population either by choice or necessity.

All the Cool Kids Are Investing

An article in the October 2013 issue of The Atlantic titled "Why Wall Street Loves Houses Again" sums up the opportunity in an article discussing the Blackstone Group's massive investment in single family housing:

"...the firm sees a new, untapped market that it believes can serve a growing group of renters who, thanks to tightening credit standards, can no longer afford the down payment to buy a home, or have been unable to convince a bank to give them a mortgage, or have simply soured on the idea of homeownership. Since the crises, Gray says the number of single-family homes being rented has increased from 11 million to 14 million. ...the downturn created an opportunity to create a business ... and in doing so we could do something for tenants that never existed before... Wouldn't somebody pay for that experience?"

My Personal Philosophy

Just a minute – just a minute. Now, hold on, Mr. Potter. Just a minute. Now, you're right when you say my father was no business man. I know that. Why he ever started this cheap, penny-ante Building and Loan, I'll never know. But neither you nor anybody else can say anything against his character, because his whole life was -- Why, in the twenty-five years since he and Uncle Billy started this thing, he never once thought of himself. Isn't that right, Uncle Billy? He didn't save enough money to send Harry to school, let alone me. But he did help a few people get outta your slums, Mr. Potter. And what's wrong with that? Why -- here, you're all businessmen here. Don't it make them better citizens? Doesn't it make them better customers?

You, you said that they -- What'd you say just a minute ago?

They had to wait and save their money before they even thought of a decent home. Wait? Wait for what?! Until their children grow up and leave them? Until they're so old and broken-down that -- You know how long it takes a workin' man to save five thousand dollars? Just remember this, Mr. Potter, that this rabble you're talking about, they do most of the working and paying and living and dying in this community. Well, is it too much to have them work and pay and live and die in a couple of decent rooms and a bath? Anyway, my father didn't think so. People were human beings to him, but to you, a warped, frustrated old man, they're cattle. Well, in my book he died a much richer man than you'll ever be.

—George Bailey's speech to Mr. Potter from the movie It's A Wonderful Life.

I have learned over the years that there is a tenant for almost every home. I have lost money over the years because I have over-improved properties for the market. I have rehabbed houses to a standard that I was comfortable with regardless of the market standard. My expectation was that if I offered a superior product in the market I would not only get above average rent, but that the tenants would appreciate it so much that they would take exceptional care of the property.

It never once worked out that way. I've lost a tremendous amount of money over the years wishing I would be rewarded for being a really good person doing the right thing. I have made the same mistakes with $350 a month units and $1000 a month units. The fact is our tenants have their own lives and worries and if they think about their landlord at all it is only when there is a problem. I get this now but it doesn't mean I don't want to offer the best product and service in every market segment. When investing in real estate it is best to check your ego at the door and look for personal validation elsewhere.

I've learned to see my responsibility as a landlord to offer safe, clean, and functional properties at a monthly rent at or just below the market. I want my tenants to feel that they are treated with respect, told the truth, and dealt with fairly. I want to be responsive to their maintenance issues especially when it comes to those items that adversely affect habitability. I want to offer the best housing I can at a price the market can afford.

The term 'slumlord' gets thrown around a lot these days. I usually hear it from people who know nothing about the business of real estate. My guess is these people feel that they are in some way supporting the relatively disadvantaged by tearing down real estate investors in general. Landlords offering affordable housing should not be generalized as slumlords any more than tenants with subsidized housing vouchers should be generalized as deadbeats. We have chosen over the years to not work with landlords who refuse to maintain their properties, just as there are prospective tenants we will never rent a property to again.

There will always be a small percentage of tenants who do not hold up their end of the landlord / tenant relationship. Some tenants abuse their status as tenants by abusing the property, by not paying the rent, or by threatening the comfort and security of others in the neighborhood. We do not hesitate to evict these people. Our job is to protect the interests of the property owners we choose to work with. We never let a few bad apples get in the way of that responsibility.

What We Believe

ROOST Real Estate Co. was founded on the premise that relationships are far more important than the individual transactions we complete. The 'why' and 'how' we do things matter. How we treat our tenants and clients matters. What we expect from ourselves and the kind of company we aspire to be matters. We think this attitude matters to the people we work with as well. In Part 7 – The Basics of Management we will delve into how we manage the myriad of daily details for our clients.

We believe that property owner profitability is a direct result of exemplary tenant relations, education, and service. Real estate investors deserve to make a significant return on their capital and ROOST brokers and agents have the expertise to help ensure that they do. At the same time, tenant clients deserve a safe and functional house or apartment that offers fair value for their money. Just as importantly, when something goes wrong they need to know that their needs will be met in a timely fashion and that all interactions will be conducted with the utmost respect.

THE ROOST PROPERTY MANAGEMENT SOLUTION

When you own investment real estate you are in the property management business. When you are in the property management business you are in the tenant relation business. While it may seem obvious it bears stating: successful tenant relations are the key to a profitable real estate business.

Are You An "Accidental" Landlord?

Did you become a real estate investor by accident? For instance, did you choose to move to a new home but decided to keep and rent your former home until the market turns around? More and more people everyday are finding themselves in this situation.

A Professional Investor?

Are you a professional investor who sees real estate as a solid long term opportunity but prefer to keep a 'hands off' approach because of a full time job and other obligations? Or, are you the type of investor who has created a business from his or her investment activities and runs this business on a part or full time basis?

Regardless of how you became a real estate investor, big or small, we can help ensure you earn the best possible return on your investment.

Do you need the services of a property manager?

Are you someone who enjoys and excels at working with tenants? Are you a natural at working the phones, solving problems, screening applicants and managing conflict? Do you like collecting rent, posting three day notices, and filing evictions when necessary? If not, our ROOST property management team can take care of it for you.

What should you expect from your property manager?

A Property Management company should offer a solution specifically tailored to your individual needs and situation. A successful relationship will allow you, the property owner, to focus on the things you do best, and delegate the things you prefer not to do to the property manager.

The Benefits of a Licensed Property Manager

The benefits of an experienced licensed property manager working for you are too numerous to mention but I expect by the time you finish this book you will have a fairly long list. A licensed property manager has a moral, legal, and fiduciary responsibility to protect your interests as your agent. They are your expert on the ground in the local market and your connection to your tenants and your property. And let me be clear, the key point here is that your property manager be licensed to practice real estate in the state they are doing business.

Being licensed is not a bonus or a 'nice' thing to have, it is the law. Only a licensed real estate broker can offer property management services for another. A real estate agent working for a real estate broker can also act as a property manager. State licensing laws help insure that your property manager is not only qualified to manage your assets, but up to date on all of the laws and regulations that affect housing, including Fair Housing laws. For a summary of licensing laws by state, visit the Institute of Real Estate Management (IREM) website at www.IREM.com.

Here is an excerpt from the IREM Property Management Licensing Report published in August of 2013:

"Most states regulate property management by including management functions such as leasing, offers to lease, negotiating leases, renting, collecting rent, etc., as covered real estate activities. In many cases, property managers who do not engage in leasing or renting activities are exempt from licensure. The typical definition of broker also specifies that these activities are being done for another individual for a fee, commission or other valuable consideration. Individuals managing their own properties are generally exempt from licensing requirements."

From the Ohio Association of Realtors (OAR) Leasing and Property Management – White Paper, July 2007 and revised in March 2014:

"Ohio Revised Code Section 4735.01(A) provides a list of activities that if performed for another for a fee requires a real estate license. This list includes anyone who "operates, manages, or rents, or offers or attempts to operate, manage, or rent other than as a custodian, caretaker, or janitor, any building or portions of buildings to the public as tenants." Also included on the list of activities that require a license are any attempts to lease property, any acts directed at procuring tenants for a property, the negotiation of leases, or advertising or holding oneself out as in the business of leasing property. Under Ohio law, performing any of these acts without a license constitutes a first degree misdemeanor and subjects the offender to a civil penalty of up to one thousand dollars per violation. Each day a violation occurs or continues is a separate violation."

The penalties for the unlicensed practice of real estate in Florida:

The crime of Unlicensed Practice of Real Estate is classified as a Third Degree Felony and assigned a Level 1 offense severity ranking under Florida's Criminal Punishment Code.

If convicted of Unlicensed Practice of Real Estate in Florida, a judge can impose any combination of the following penalties:

- Up to five (5) years in prison.
- Up to five (5) years of probation.
- Up to $5,000 in fines.

Here is a summary of activities that and unlicensed individual can and cannot do published by the OAR Daily Buzz May 2015:

"Ohio license law contains a rule which answers these questions for residential property management. Ohio Administrative Code Section 1301:5-5-07 provides a list of activities that an unlicensed person can and cannot perform with regard to residential property management. The rule also provides that the unlicensed individual performing the permitted activities listed in this rule must work under the supervision of a broker and his/her compensation must be primarily on a salaried or hourly basis.

Under this rule, the duties an unlicensed employee can perform when working with residential rental property are the following:

- maintenance
- clerical or administrative support
- collect or accept rents and/or security deposits which are made payable to the owner or real estate brokerage
- exhibit or show residential rental units to prospective tenants
- furnish published information regarding the property
- supply applications and leases
- receive applications and leases for submission to the owner or broker for approval

The rule provides that an unlicensed employee may not perform the following duties:

- negotiate contracts or leases
- deviate from the rental price and/or other terms and conditions previously established by the owner or broker when providing information to prospective tenants
- approve rental applications or leases
- settle or arrange the terms and conditions of a lease on behalf of the owner or broker
- offer inducements to prospective tenants unless they are previously advertised or arranged with the owner or broker

- interpret or provide their opinion concerning the terms or conditions of a lease

- indicate to the public that he is in a position of authority which has the ultimate managerial responsibility of the rental property

It's clear that a brokerage employee can perform many clerical and administrative functions without holding a real estate license. They can provide information to prospective tenants, show units and supply and accept tenant applications and leases. However, unlicensed employees cannot act as the property manager or function as a "decision maker." Instead, performing that role is limited to a real estate licensee.

It is also important to note that the above rule applies only to residential property management. The licensure exemption does not apply to commercial, industrial or retail property management, or in real estate sales of any type.

Brokers engaged in property management must understand what activities their unlicensed employees can perform and provide clear guidance to their employees regarding the duties they are permitted to perform under Ohio law. It is the broker's responsibility to make sure that their employees do not cross over this line and perform activities limited to only licensed agents."

This is important information to have when interviewing, evaluating and selecting a property management firm.

An Unlicensed Property Manager Horror Story

A new client contacted us unexpectedly a few years ago with close to 70 single family homes in Springfield, Ohio they needed help with. They were from upstate New York and had purchased these properties over a 24 month period through a buyer's agent based in a county just north of ours. As far as I know, they never saw the properties before they bought them. They had learned via the internet that Springfield, Ohio had some of the cheapest housing stock in the nation so they were confident in their purchases.

These owners were not the only ones enticed by our 'bargains'. We have worked with buyers from California, Washington and from Canada as well. They all thought they were going to get rich quickly because the asking prices of houses here were a fraction of what property was selling for in their home towns. They all bought their properties without consulting a local professional, and they all came to us after their business plans fell apart. These buyers all failed to consider the condition of the properties they were buying and the true cost of the initial rehab and ongoing upkeep and repair. They also consistently over-estimated the amount of rent they could collect and the number of months each year they should expect to collect it. They did not necessarily overpay for their houses, but they overestimated their profit margins.

Almost all of these owners initially assumed they could manage their properties themselves from a distance. As I have written earlier, lower and moderate priced scattered lot single family housing requires a hands on approach to day to day operations that managing from a distance does not allow. To their credit, our friends from New York did hire a property manager to help them. Their mistake was hiring an unlicensed individual as their manager and by the time we got involved they had lost tens of thousands of dollars.

I have not bought a house yet for under $20,000 that did not require at least some repairs, and most require fairly extensive upgrades. The upgrades almost always involve big ticket items like roofs and windows. Our out of state owner discovered this truth as well. Our new clients were introduced to a local contractor who starting rehabbing the properties. Before long the contractor had volunteered to help find tenants, collect rent, and do ongoing maintenance and repairs. This sounded like a terrific arrangement and things went along just fine at first.

Things eventually fell apart because there was no tenant screening or selection process in place for new tenants. There were other reasons too but this was the big one. By the time we got involved barely half the properties were occupied and the tenants in half of those were not paying rent and in need of eviction. The owners were understandably angry and frustrated. I am sure the manager, who was essentially a one person operation, was feeling overwhelmed and taken advantage of as well.

While our owners did lose a lot of money in rent, where they really got killed was in the cost of repairs and rehabs. While their loyalty to their manger was admirable, it was their manager who was doing the construction work. Not only was there no competitive bidding going on, but from what we could tell the manager was billing the owners at a very substantial mark-up. This was in addition to the compensation he was collecting as a percentage of the rent and security deposits collected.

The unlicensed manger was the only person making money on these houses. Somewhat unbelievably, we found instances where work was done on houses that should have been torn down. We found truly terrible, uninhabitable houses in very tough locations with new roofs on them. It would have been hard to prove that the manger's actions were fraudulent or criminal. The owners were after all paying him. He may have been incompetent, but the owners supported his actions by giving him a free hand.

We do know that under Ohio law, acting as a property manager without a license constitutes a first degree misdemeanor and subjects the offender to a civil penalty of up to one thousand dollars per violation. Had the manger been reported to the Ohio Division of Real Estate, observed, charged, prosecuted and found guilty, he would have owed thousands of dollars in fines.

Fortunately for our owner, this story has a happy ending, but there are several lessons to be learned here. The first lesson is you cannot manage property on your own from a distance. The second is you need to have a set of basic standards for your property manager, including being licensed. And three, one should at least spend the amount of time and effort to select a property manager that one would spend to qualify a new tenant. A good property manager will make you money far beyond the fee you will pay them.

Whether you are an Accidental Landlord or a Professional Investor, ROOST™ will help insure that your real estate investment works for you, and not the other way around.

Here is a sampling of activities we manage on a daily basis:

- Rehabbing, painting and renovating.
- Performing preventative maintenance.
- Marketing and advertising vacancies.
- Screening potential tenants.
- Writing leases and keeping track of files and paperwork.
- Keeping the books.
- Answering emergency calls and tenant inquiries.
- Answering ad calls generated from ads placed in the paper.
- Mediating tenant disputes.
- Collecting rent.
- Posting notices, filing evictions and going to court.
- Consulting with our owner clients to help improve their ROI.

Let us do what we do best so you can focus on what you do best. We will tailor a ROOST Property Management Solution to meet your unique needs.

The ROOST Landlord Advantage™

The ROOST Way™

Prospective tenants across a wide spectrum of price points look to ROOST Real Estate Co.™ for available apartments and homes to rent. Tenants and Owners both benefit from the policies and expectations outlined in The ROOST Way™ a comprehensive guide to being a successful tenant.

The Advertising Solution

All of our available inventory can be viewed online via computer or mobile device at :
www.ROOSTRentals4U.com
www.ROOSTRealEstateCo.com and on literally hundreds of rental property sites including Zillow and Apartments.com.

The Tenant Selection Process

Our application process includes a criminal background, credit, and reference check. We look for prior evictions and verify employment. We require applicants to produce pay stubs to verify their income. We supply all of the paperwork and disclosures necessary to comply with all local, state and federal Fair Housing laws.

The Rent Maximizer

Your success as a real estate investor depends on positive tenant relationships. Our staff understands the importance of retaining your existing tenants as well as attracting new ones. However, our policy is that rent is due on the 1st, late on the 5th and we post 3-day eviction notices by the 10th. We work with our tenants whenever we can and will even get them in touch various relief organizations when appropriate, however, we maintain this standard at all times.

The Team Advantage

Our property management team includes a licensed Tenant Relations Manager and an experienced staff of assistants, receptionists, bookkeepers, accounting and information technology professionals. We are available from 9:00am to 6:00pm Monday through Friday and Saturday from 10:00am to 1:00pm to accommodate the needs of our tenants. Our office is conveniently located in the heart of downtown Springfield.

The Tenant Service Standard

We have a talented and capable staff of maintenance people available for routine and preventative work. After hours emergency maintenance is available as well. Our standard is to complete routine requests within 72 hours and to stay in touch with the tenant throughout the process.

The Profitability Snapshot

We employ an internet based property management system which allows owners access to information about their properties 24 hours a day. We can disperse proceeds monthly, quarterly, or annually based on positive cash flow.

The Value Proposition

We are licensed by the state of Ohio to perform property management services. We tailor our services to the unique needs of our individual clients. We charge a nominal set up fee to assess and integrate your properties into our system. We charge a straight percentage of collected rent and a separate fee for each new lease signed or lease renewed. There are no charges for vacant units. (Multiple unit discounts are available.)

Our Message to Prospective Tenants

We call the unique experience we offer our tenant clients The ROOST Way™. Our marketing brochures and websites outline what our prospective tenants can expect from us as well as what we expect from them. We need our tenants to be successful and our owners need our tenants to be successful. Securing a high success rate involves some education and handholding on our part. That is why we make our value proposition as explicit and easy to understand as we can.

To Our Future Clients

Whether you are looking for your first apartment or your next apartment, at ROOST we want you to be 100% satisfied with your rental experience. We want you to get the most value possible for your monthly rent payment. We also want to do such a good job for you that you are always happy to refer your friends, family, and coworkers to ROOST for all of their real estate needs.

At ROOST Real Estate Co. we work by referral, and we are constantly striving to earn yours.

The ultimate goal of The ROOST Way™ is not only to provide you with a great place to live, but to ensure that your rental experience benefits you financially. For many this may be as simple as being able to afford the rent, avoiding late fees, and ensuring that you receive your full security deposit at the end of the lease term. For others, it may mean using the lease term to prepare to purchase a home of their own.

Whatever your goals, The ROOST Way™ is all about supporting the way you want to live today, and setting the stage for how you may want to live tomorrow.

Sincerely,

Chris McAllister

Chris McAllister / ROOST Real Estate Co.

The ROOST Way™

The Pick Me Application

First things first, bring us a complete application including your last couple of pay stubs so we can verify that you can afford the home or apartment you are interested in. A complete and accurate application will ensure that we can get you a decision promptly.

The ROOST Reference Check

We do a credit and criminal background check for all of our applicants. We also check the references you provide us, so make sure you cross your 'I's and so on. Please give us working phone numbers for your references, past landlords, and employers. This will help ensure your application goes to the top of our waiting list.

The Certified Rental Home

We perform a detailed inspection of every home and apartment we rent to ensure that it is ready for you the day you move in. We will review the inspection with you when you sign your lease. We want your experience with us to start off right on day one.

The Pet Plan

We allow up to two cats and a single dog (excluding breeds restricted by our insurance company) in many of our single family homes. You should plan to pay an additional non-refundable security deposit and a monthly Pet Fee in addition to your regular rent. We are sorry, but pets are not allowed in multi-family or apartment buildings. Pets in buildings with common areas interferes with the quiet enjoyment of the premises by the other tenants.

The Utility Solution

If you are renting a single family home you will be required to have the utilities placed in your name. This includes gas, electric, water and trash pickup. Multi-unit and apartment buildings will have the water and trash pick-up included in your rent. Some of our owners will allow you to include your utilities in with your rent with an additional security deposit. If you are unable to secure utilities in your name at the time you sign your lease, this may be a good solution for you.

The Never Pay Late Secret

The most important thing you can do to ensure a successful relationship with ROOST Real Estate Co. is to pay your rent on time. The secret is to work on getting a month ahead on your rent so that if you do have an emergency you will not have to worry as much when the first of the month comes around. We are happy to help you track any advance payments you would like to make to build up a credit on your account.

The 'Fix It' Request

There is nothing more frustrating than having something broken in your home and not being able to get it fixed. We understand and are dedicated to responding to your maintenance requests in a timely fashion and taking care of emergency situations right away.

The Move Out Walk Through

When it does come time to move to a new apartment or home, we want to make sure you receive your full security deposit. First of all, be sure to give a full 30 day written notice to us that you are moving out. Second, be sure that you paid all of your rent on time including your last month and any outstanding late fees or additional charges. Third, make sure your home is in as good or better shape as it was when you moved in. This will guarantee that you receive your full deposit back as quickly as possible and a terrific reference from ROOST Real Estate Co. as well.

The My First ROOST™ Program

While we would love to have you rent from ROOST for years to come, we have a plan called My First ROOST™ designed to help first time homebuyers regardless of their credit situation work towards getting qualified for mortgage. A ROOST Realtor will personally sit down with you and take you through the entire process of buying a house and stick by you the whole way, regardless of how long it takes.

A word about Pets

Some of our owner clients do not want any pets in their homes. Depending on the home in question this may be appropriate. Our feeling is pets should not be allowed in high density apartment complexes period. We discourage owners from allowing dogs in doubles in duplexes but generally we allow a cat with an additional deposit and monthly fee. In most single family homes we allow pets. However, we need to see a picture of the animal if not the animal itself, and again, an additional deposit and monthly fee is required.

What does ROOST expect from you?

It is simple really. A landlord wants to be able to make their monthly mortgage, tax, insurance and utility payments on time. They don't want any complaints from the neighbors or other tenants regarding excessive noise or bad behavior. Most importantly, they want you to take care of your home and when your lease is up, leave it in the same or better condition than when you moved in.

What should you expect from ROOST?

You should expect a clean, functional unit that is move in condition the day your sign your lease. You should expect a staff that is responsive to your needs should your home require maintenance or repairs. Finally, you should expect to be treated at all times with the utmost respect.

Here are a few of the calls we take so you don't have to.

"When applying, is there a limit to how many evictions you can have?"

"I can't pay my rent because someone stole my refrigerator."

"I can't take my trash out because I have a baby."

"The health department called because there is a turkey in the backyard eating trash".

"The ants are eating my neighbor's eyelids."

"My son died." - Then the son called...

"There's a squirrel on my head in my bedroom, and it sounds like he's got kids with him"

"I'm going to prison next month so I won't be able to pay September's rent."

"Is this house still available to rent? My wife is about to die and I want to move in there with my girlfriend."

To the judge - "I have a rare brain disease that makes me forget things. So I forgot to pay rent."

LONG TERM TRENDS FAVOR LAND-LORD/INVESTORS - MARCH 2009

I have been taken with the writings and musings of Richard Florida lately. Check out his blog at www.creativeclass.com. In a recent article he wrote for The Atlantic Monthly, entitled "How the Crash Will Reshape America", Florida opines on how we got here, trends we should be aware of, and the opportunities that await.

Florida argues that homeownership should be removed from its "privileged place at the center of the U.S. economy". Tax breaks and artificially low interest rates encourage people to buy more home than they otherwise would. The result is that less is spent in other areas of the economy that would drive long term growth and prosperity. When more is spent on housing, by individuals and government in the form of tax breaks and low interest rates, less is spent/invested in medical technology, software or alternative energy solutions.

Given that people need to be more mobile to respond to career opportunities, Florida believes that the government should encourage renting rather than buying. In addition, research has shown that homeowners are generally no happier than renters, and experience no less stress and no greater self-esteem.

I have made this point before, but it bears repeating; we have to stop equating homeownership with the "pursuit of happiness' aspect of the American Dream.

There are some intangible and social benefits to homeownership. Pride in one's home translates into caring for one's neighborhood, and ties to a specific location aid in civic loyalty and involvement. However, these benefits come at a great cost to the overall economy and our individual well-being.

The economist Andrew Oswald claims his research shows that areas with higher homeownership suffer higher unemployment. (This makes sense; if you can't leave your home to go where the work is, you may not work.) Oswald shows that homeownership is a more important predictor of unemployment than unionization rates or quantity or quality of welfare benefits available.

The truth is that homeownership links people to declining economic areas and forces them into unemployment or long term underemployment. Admittedly, growing up and living in the rust belt of America may have left me jaded. However, what about the boom towns of the last decade? Who will live in the vacant housing stock in Nevada, Arizona or Florida if the jobs are not there?

Florida goes on to mention that as homeownership rates have risen, 'our society has become less nimble'. Americans were nearly twice as likely to move in the '50s and '60s as they are today. During 2008, fewer Americans moved as a percentage of the population than at any time since the 1940s. Many homeowners are stuck where they are, regardless of where gainful employment may be available.

In my opinion, the American Dream is about the opportunity to pursue your highest and best work or achievement. Homeownership as a central tenant of America's economic and social paradigms is inconsistent with 21st century reality and individual pursuits of happiness. So what is the solution?

The government should make it easier for people to leave their homes behind and start fresh where they want to live. Private investors should be brought in to take over and manage these properties at today's market value. On the other side, investors need to make rental property available to new workers in the next likely 'boom' towns – places like Silicon Valley, Boulder, Austin and the Carolinas. Individuals, employers, the government, and private real estate investors will need to work together to create a new housing standard where people are encouraged to rent if that is in their best interest.

A new housing and economic paradigm with a greater emphasis on serving those who should rent rather than buy will help the individual and benefit the overall economy. Fortunately, these trends bode well for landlords and real estate investors. It will not be easy, and it will be messy. But honestly, who believes we are going back to the boom years of 2002 to 2005? Now is the time to buy while foreclosures are plentiful – it is also the time to hold onto rental property in anticipation of a cultural shift that is happening as we speak.

It is a great time to be a real estate investor. The opportunities are becoming clearer and clearer as we move through this housing and lending crises. Things are really starting to get interesting right about now.

OWNER PROFITABILITY IS JOB #1

PART 4: OWNER PROFITABILITY IS JOB #1

My definition of real estate investing is buying and renting for the long term. Flipping is also considered investing by most people, but I consider flipping houses to be a construction or construction management business. Flipping is 100% about buying a property at the right price, completing any necessary repairs and upgrades as quickly and cost effectively as possible, and then selling to the highest bidder.

In my mind, flipping houses carries more financial risk and pressure than buying and renting; but that does not mean selling a property from time to time doesn't make sense. If you can cash out a property and use the proceeds to invest in a new property with a greater return, then yes, by all means sell. My investing strategy is about taking the long view—and I buy for cash flow and not short term gains.

Investing in real estate is different from investing in other asset classes like stocks and bonds because it is not liquid. Prior to 2008 and 2009, real estate was considered to be a 'stable' investment. Unlike stocks and bonds, price volatility was minimal. It was much easier to anticipate the value of a piece of property in the short term, say three to six months, in 2006 than it is in 2016.

Today, there are many more external forces that can affect housing in the short and medium term. In our hyper-connected financial, social, and 24 hour a day news world, a hiccup in another country can affect or delay the sale of your flip house. When flipping property, especially if financing is involved, every day on the market costs money.

People's reactions to news may not be rational, but we all consider either consciously or subconsciously how and to what degree an unexpected event will affect our jobs. From a buyer's perspective, committing to a 30 year mortgage is a big deal, and harder to do if there is even a chance that your income could be in jeopardy. Yes, I may be overly cautious at this stage of my life, but this allows me to be less concerned about the short and medium term market value of my property.

In this chapter, I am going to show you how to value a property based on cash flow. I am also going to discuss all of the obvious, and not so obvious costs and expenses you may encounter in your investing activities. More importantly, I am going to give you a profit formula and evaluation method that anticipates these costs.

The 'Wal-Mart' Client

When I talk about "The Wal-Mart Client," I am basically referring to the Best Case Springfield, Ohio Rental Applicant. Springfield is classic rust-belt working class town with a large number of rental properties and tenants. We are steadily losing population as our manufacturing base continues to shrink. A 'good' job here does not pay much money.

Springfield, and sadly most of Southern Ohio outside of the Columbus and Cincinnati areas, continue to struggle economically. Manufacturing jobs have virtually disappeared, and high tech jobs have yet to gain any sort of foothold. Our incomes are down and unemployment is up. This means that the majority of working individuals in our market can afford around $450 a month in rent. If your cost structure allows you to charge rent in this area, you will find a broader pool of applicants from which to select your next tenant.

Our preferred tenant is someone who makes between $350 and $400 a week. I use the description of a Wal-Mart Supervisor making $8.50 to $10.00 hour and averaging 35 hours a week. This person may not make a lot of money but they work for a very stable company. Many health care, call center, and fast food workers fall into this category as well. These people may still require some form of public assistance, but they have steady employment.

$9.00 an hour at 35 hours a week translates to $1365 a month gross income. We look for our applicants to make at least three times the rent amount in monthly income. $1,365 translates to a target monthly rent figure of $455. Obviously, if you can afford to rent your unit for $400 vs. $500, you will have a better shot at collecting rent 10 to 12 months out of the year versus less than 10 or not collecting any rent at all.

Our goal therefore is to buy and maintain property that we can cash flow at these income levels. Furthermore, by expanding the number of applicants we have to choose from, the better chance we have of finding a tenant most likely to pay the rent and maintain the property throughout the lease term.

TWO CASE STUDIES

Here are two of my investments that illustrate tenants and properties that fit the 'Wal-Mart Client' scenario. The first is a single family home, and the second is an up and down duplex. Both of these properties have been consistently profitable for me.

CASE STUDY #1
WEST WASHINGTON STREET

Single Family Home

PURCHASE PRICE:		$5,000.00
Rehab:		$17,685.00
TOTAL INVESTMENT:		$22,685.00

POTENTIAL RENT:	**MONTHLY**	**ANNUALLY**
Unit 1:	$495.00	$5,940.00
Unit 2::	$0.00	$0.00
TOTAL:	$495.00	$5,940.00

Vacancy Reserve 10%:	-$49.50	-$594.00
Repair Reserve 20%:	-$99.00	-$1,188.00
Insurance:	-$45.00	-$540.00
Property Taxes:	-$13.00	-$156.00
Interest Expense:	$0.00	$0.00
Water:	$0.00	$0.00
Trash/$18 Per Unit:	$0.00	$0.00
Mowing/Average Over 12 Months:	$0.00	$0.00
Professional Management 10%	-$49.50	-$594.00
TOTAL EXPENSES:	-$256.00	-$3,072.00

NET PROFIT:	$239.00	$2,868.00
Estimated Appreciation:		0.00%

ANNUAL ROI:		12.64%

This house has done very well for me. I bought it right, managed the rehab effectively, and the property taxes are very reasonable. It rents well at $495 a month, and most importantly to me, it generates comfortable repair and vacancy reserves. It does not quite hit my 15% return on investment (ROI) target, but it is a great property for me. I will discuss determining reasonable ROI targets later in this chapter.

CASE STUDY #2
WEST
HIGH STREET

Up and Down Duplex

PURCHASE PRICE:		$5,500.00
Rehab:		$9,666.00
TOTAL INVESTMENT:		$15,166.00
POTENTIAL RENT:	**MONTHLY**	**ANNUALLY**
Unit 1:	$268.00	$3,216.00
Unit 2::	$375.00	$4,500.00
TOTAL:	**$643.00**	**$7,716.00**
Vacancy Reserve 10%:	-$64.30	-$771.60
Repair Reserve 20%:	-$128.60	-$1,543.20
Insurance:	-$50.00	-$600.00
Property Taxes:	-$28.00	-$336.00
Interest Expense:	$0.00	$0.00
Water:	-$35.00	$420.00
Trash/$18 Per Unit:	-$36.00	-$432.00
Mowing/Average Over 12 Months:	-$35.00	-$420.00
Professional Management 10%	-$64.30	-$771.60
TOTAL EXPENSES:	**-$441.20**	**-$5,294.40**
NET PROFIT:	**$201.80**	**$2,421.60**
Estimated Appreciation:		0.00%
ANNUAL ROI:		**15.97%**

As a rule I prefer single family and side by side doubles to up and down duplexes, but this house is a happy exception to my rule.

Know Your Market

As an investor, you must be crystal clear on the specifics of the market you are operating in. There may be a market segment or group of potential customers whose needs are not being met in your area. If you can identify those customers and service them profitably, you will be successful. Whether you are planning to serve working class families, students, urban professionals, empty nesters, or any other potential tenant group, it helps to have a thorough understanding of what they are looking for, and what they can afford to pay before you dive in.

Stakeholders to Consider

There are other constituencies besides your tenants to consider when investing in real estate. These groups can adversely affect your cash flow if you fail to acknowledge their needs and wants. They can also help you when you need them. The most demanding of these constituencies are generally local government agencies.

It is easy to dismiss local government employees as bureaucrats simply looking to justify their existence by making their presence and importance known. There are a few bad apples out there, and they can be a nuisance and a detriment to your business; however, the vast majority of these public servants have a job to do, and they do it well. It is also important to remember that the rules and regulations they are paid to enforce were at least initially designed to protect tenants and owners, as well as the community at large.

The Section 8 Housing Voucher Program

One of the main local government entities we interact with regularly are the people who run the Section 8 Housing Voucher program. We rent approximately 10% of the housing we manage to tenants who are getting assistance from Section 8. (For a full description of what the Section 8 program is all about visit http://portal.hud.gov.)

Section 8 will pay up to 100% of the approved monthly rent amount for a qualified applicant. The money is direct deposited into our property management trust account on the first of every month. This is of course a wonderful thing. However, an applicant with a Section 8 voucher does not automatically get to rent through us. Just like anyone else, they must go through the application and screening process, and many times we choose not to rent to them based on their past rental history, landlord references or criminal background.

Section 8 determines the maximum rent they will approve for a house based on the number of bedrooms it has. In my experience, the Section 8 maximum rent guidelines are very fair, but they do restrict tenants to lower income neighborhoods. No landlord that I know would rent to a family with a Section 8 voucher if the approved rent were less than market value. If you work in lower income areas like we do, the program has a lot to offer.

Having said that, some owners refuse to work with Section 8 on principle. In exchange for regular rent over the term of the lease, the home has to meet their minimum standards for safety, functionality and security. While the vast majority of our owners expect their properties to meet these minimum standards anyway, some simply don't like being told what to do and when to do it.

There are also some deviations among Section 8 inspectors. Some inspectors are more 'picky' than others and this sometimes means additional repair requests are made that another inspector may not ask for. The inconsistencies can be frustrating and a primary reason why some owners refuse to work with the program.

In our experience, like everything else in this business, it comes down to relationships. We strive to develop positive and productive relationships with everyone who works at Section 8. They know we respect the job they do and what it takes to do it, and they in turn respect what we do. That is the key to success in the program.

Code Enforcement

Most municipalities have a code enforcement division. The Code Enforcement Division of the City of Springfield is part of the building and zoning department. Code Enforcement ensures that the grass gets mowed, weeds and brush are removed and the trash gets picked up throughout the city. They do many other things including taking complaints from angry tenants and doing property inspections to follow up on any mandated repairs that may result from a tenant dispute.

Our leases for single-family homes stipulate that the tenant is responsible for maintaining the yard and the trash pick-up. In a multi-unit building, the landlord is responsible for these items. Springfield is the only city of its size that I know of in America that does not provide trash service. In our city, each property owner must contract with one of three or four licensed private hauling firms for trash pickup. If a tenant gets behind on their bill, the trash does not get picked up.

As you can imagine, this privatization of public services, which occurred over 20 years ago has resulted in all sorts of unintended consequences. For instance all the trash haulers run identical routes all over town duplicating efforts and wasting resources. Second, it is not just tenants that sometimes don't pay their trash bills. Owner occupants are not all perfect either. The result is abandoned trash in vacant lots and yards all over town, but especially in the more depressed and lower income areas. Code Enforcement is responsible for making sure all of the abandoned trash is dealt with and that ultimate financial responsibility falls on the property owner.

Obviously this situation could be vastly improved if all property owners were billed for trash pickup on their water bills. The city could still use private haulers, but all would share the cost. In any case, our property managers have a positive and productive relationship with Code Enforcement. They know if there is an issue with one of our properties we will take care of it. Consequently, if an issue arises, we generally get a courtesy call before a formal citation is issued. Again, the relationship here is paramount.

The Water Department

The local water department can be your best friend or a detriment to your business. Water bills 'run with the property'. This means, like property taxes, they are the responsibility of the property owner. While the lease may stipulate that the tenant is responsible for the water bill, if they don't pay it the owner of record is responsible.

Recovering damages involves billing back the tenant, or in an extreme situation, evicting them and recovering the costs from their security deposit. Practically, you want a relationship with someone at the department that will alert you if there is a problem, and in the case of vacant properties, get the water turned on and off as necessary in a timely fashion.

Landlord Tenant Agreements with the Gas and Electric Companies

We set up what are called landlord agreements with our local gas and electric companies. These are designed so that if a tenant moves out without telling us, or fails to pay their monthly bills and their service is cut off, the account reverts to us the property manager. This is critical in the winter time when the danger of pipes freezing and then breaking when they thaw is a clear and present danger. A broken pipe with water running can cause catastrophic property losses for an owner.

The State or Local Health Department

You may also find yourself interacting with your county health department. Our county health department is responsible for ensuring well and septic systems are safe and maintained to code. If you have a home in the country, they can be a wealth of help and information should you have a water or septic system problem. Your local or state health department may also be responsible for investigating any reports of lead paint exposure by your tenants. Again, these entities offer a wealth of information to help you anticipate and prevent problems that can impact your profitability.

Be a Good Neighbor

Being on good terms with the neighborhood is also important. Your neighbors can make or break your investment. If you take care of your property and any problem tenants you may have promptly, generally you will be rewarded with good 'press' and your house will be looked after and protected. Your pride of ownership will be rewarded.

Insurance

Another cost to consider and manage is insurance. An insurance agent that specializes in working with real estate investors is critical to your success. At a minimum, you want to carry liability insurance, which covers you if someone is hurt on your property. This is generally very inexpensive at less than $15 a month in my experience.

Some of our clients are 'self-insured'. Meaning they may pay for liability insurance, but they do not have any other coverage on their properties. This means they personally absorb any losses that may occur. If you have a mortgage on a property, your lender will specify the minimum amount of coverage they require. This approach is obviously risky, and I would never recommend it to my clients.

Property Taxes

Property taxes are a fact of life. However, they too can be managed if the county's assessment of the value of the property is unreasonable. In Ohio, a property owner can appeal his or her taxes to the county Board of Revision between January 1 and March 31 of each year. If you can show that your property is over-valued, you may be able to have the assessed value reduced, which will reduce your property tax liability.

What you paid for the property is considered fair value if the transaction was at arm's length. In Ohio, arm's length transactions do not include 'distressed' sales including short sales and sales of bank foreclosures. However, if you have a certified appraisal of the property that supports your value, or can show that current assessed values of like properties in the area are less than yours, you may be able to obtain some relief. In my experience, it is worth a try.

Your Occupancy Rate

When planning for an occupancy rate, I try to anticipate how many months a year that I can count on collecting rent. Obviously, there is a difference between someone occupying a property and paying rent. You would be surprised how many owners tell us they are 100% occupied but are not coming close to collecting 100% of their potential rent. You may also be surprised at how many people buy investment property with the assumption that it will never be vacant. That is what I call Magical Thinking, but I digress.

On a lower end property, and depending on our experience in the neighborhood, I may only budget for collecting rent 10 months of the year. This means I am planning on collecting rent—worst case 83% of the year. (10 months/12 months = 83.33%) I will round down a bit and say my vacancy rate will be 15%. So if my monthly potential or market rate rent is $500 a month, or $6000 a year, I build my budget with the understanding that I am only going to collect 85% of that, or $5,100 a year.

On average, I plan to collect rent 90% of the time and to be vacant 10% of the time. This equates to successfully collecting rent roughly 11 times every 12-month period. It is virtually impossible to collect rent every month during the life of an investment. Even if a tenant stays in a house for two full years, it is very likely that you will miss at least one month's rent between tenants and likely two depending on the time of year and the time it takes to prepare the home for the next tenant. One vacant month out of 24 means a 95% occupancy rate and two out of 24 brings us back to 90%.

The Eviction Process

At some point you will have a tenant that fails, for whatever reason, to pay their rent. It is important to stress with your tenant at the start of the relationship that the rent is always due in your office on the first of every month, and if it is not there by the fifth, they are subject to both late fees and an eviction. Our philosophy is rent is due on the first, and if we don't have it by the morning of the sixth day of the month, they can expect an eviction notice to be posted on the property giving them three days to move out. After the three days have passed, we have the right to file the eviction with the local municipal court.

I know what you are thinking—nice people don't evict people. We consider our owners to be nice people too, and they deserve a consistent return on their investment. Having said that, if we have good history with a tenant, and if they are upfront about their situation and have a plan to get current, we will bend the policy with the owner's consent. In most cases however, we start the eviction process while at the same time suggesting possible sources of financial help in the community that the tenant may be able to turn to.

For most people, having to evict a tenant is the most distasteful part of being a landlord. Failure to carry out an eviction in a timely manner however, will negatively impact your return. In our experience, if we act early in the month and put the eviction process in motion, we can usually get a court date early the following month and have possession of the house soon after that. Best case, our landlords will lose two months' rent. If we hesitate just a few days however, we can easily lose three months' rent.

In our county, filing an eviction costs $130.00 in court costs, and we have an attorney that works with us that charges $125 for his signature on the court documents. A writ of possession and a visit from the sheriff is another $25.00. Our property managers file the eviction and attend eviction court. We do not charge extra for this service, but we do pass along the $280.00 in court costs and attorney fees to our owners.

The majority of the time the tenant will come up with the money owed in addition to the court costs and attorney fees and remain in the property. Maybe a third of the time they vacate the property on their own prior to the court date. Once in a while the tenant will remain in the property up until the bailiff and the sheriff arrive to execute the writ of possession. At that time they are escorted off the premises. That, as you can imagine, is never pleasant, but it is one of the things you pay a property manager to do.

Late Fees

Some of our owners stipulate a late fee of $5.00 a day after the fifth of the month, and others charge a flat percentage of the monthly rent after the fifth. The idea is to discourage tenants from taking their time getting the rent in each month. The late fees also compensate the owner for late income they may need to meet their monthly obligations. Unpaid late fees are deducted from the tenant's security deposit at the end of the lease term.

Repairs and Maintenance

No matter what you plan for repairs and maintenance it will likely not be enough. I budget 20% of collected rent. Many people feel this is excessive, but in my experience it is the minimum acceptable reserve. Not every property I own costs me 20%, but a few will cost me far more.

By applying this percentage across all of my properties, I am usually not surprised and almost never caught short. If I have

50 properties renting for an average of $500 a month that is $25,000 a month in gross income. 20% of that figure is $5,000 or $60,000 over the course of the year to cover labor and materials. If I don't need all of it any given year, it is additional profit to me that I can use for new properties or upgrades to existing properties. The next chapter of this book deals exclusively with maintenance and repairs.

Professional Management

I have used 10% of collected rent for 'Professional Management' fees in each of my case studies. As you are aware by now, this entire book is about the importance of professional management to your profitability as a real estate investor. While our base fees are 10% of collected rent, we do provide discounts for large apartment complexes and larger scattered lot portfolios. I like to err on the high side when forecasting expenses, which I have done throughout this book.

Valuing a Property

For the record, single-family homes will rent towards the high side (and higher) of the local rent range. Side-by-side doubles will rent for less, duplexes (units above and below each other) will rent for even less, and three to four units in a single building will often rent for less still. Single-family homes obviously should cost more to purchase on a per unit basis than a multi-unit building costs.

When considering property to purchase, our goal is to provide good shelter for a price that is affordable for a substantial portion of the population. The following is a dissertation on determining the investment value of a property based on Return on Investment or ROI. Let's look at the ROI of another one of my Springfield properties.

CASE STUDY #3
COLUMBUS AVENUE

Single Family Home

PURCHASE PRICE:		$12,000.00
Rehab:		$4,538.00
TOTAL INVESTMENT:		**$16,538.00**

POTENTIAL RENT:	MONTHLY	ANNUALLY
Unit 1:	$565.00	$6,780.00
Unit 2::	$0.00	$0.00
TOTAL:	**$565.00**	**$6,780.00**
Vacancy Reserve 10%:	-$56.50	-$678.00
Repair Reserve 20%:	-$113.00	-$1,356.00
Insurance:	-$50.00	-$600.00
Property Taxes:	-$28.00	-$540.00
Interest Expense:	$0.00	$0.00
Water:	$0.00	$0.00
Trash/$18 Per Unit:	$0.00	$0.00
Mowing/Average Over 12 Months:	$0.00	$0.00
Professional Management 10%	-$56.50	-$678.00
TOTAL EXPENSES:	**-$321.00**	**-$3,852.00**
NET PROFIT:	**$244.00**	**$2,928.00**
Estimated Appreciation:		0.00%
ANNUAL ROI:		**17.70%**

This property has averaged a 17%+ return every year that I have owned it. Only in fairly depressed markets am I going to be able to buy properties that perform this well. When I consider any property to buy in Springfield, my goal is to achieve 20% ROI, but I am happy if I average 15% to 17% after all expenses. So again, I will not buy anything unless I think I have a shot at 20% but I am happy with anything above 15%. I have also included some case studies later in this chapter where I don't hit 15%. In every case, it is because I spent more on the rehab than I planned. Overall however, I have built a portfolio that exceeds a 15% return overall, after all expenses, including management.

When evaluating a property to purchase, you must first do an analysis based on what you think the rental performance will be. This is called a pro-forma. Determining market rate rent is fairly easy these days. You can get a good idea by perusing rental websites and even Zillow.com. Just remember to make sure that you are comparing rental rates in similar blocks and neighborhoods.

The second step is to determine your target ROI. In Springfield, that target may be 15% to 20%, but realistically in an appreciating market 10% may be a spectacular return. In a place like Melbourne, Florida, anything over 6% is a win. In Melbourne however, market values are going up by over 6% a year. The recent appreciation history and near to medium term potential (one to three years) has to be considered when you set your ROI targets.

In the previous case study, we calculated my ROI based on the forecasted profit and on the amount of money invested in the property. What I have invested in the property is a hard number. There is no estimating involved. It is what it is. My expected profit on the property is based on past performance that should continue in the future. In this case study, we know both sides of the equation and can easily calculate ROI.

What if we have no history for a property but we need to estimate its value? The only hard number we have at this point is our target ROI. However, we can estimate what kind of profit the property will generate based on a market analysis and our past experience. So, if we have an ROI target and a profit estimate, we can calculate what the property is worth to us.

Let's say a property owner comes to you and says he has a house in Cincinnati, Ohio that he wants to sell. He tells you to "Take a look at it and make me an offer." Knowing that this area of Cincinnati is hot right now and rents are rising, you tell him you would be happy to take a look. You expect to make an all cash offer for the property.

Once inside you see that the house is in good shape but needs $10,000 or so in cosmetic updates. You figure that with these updates you should be able to rent the property for $1,200 a month. Your internet search of similar homes for rent in the area confirms your estimate.

There is so much demand in this area that you can forecast a vacancy rate of only 5%. The home has no carpet, just hardwood floors throughout, and after your initial rehab, the ongoing maintenance should be minimal. Based on this, you feel comfortable budgeting repair and maintenance costs at 10% of the collected rent. Your analysis looks like this:

CASE STUDY #4
CINCINNATI HYPOTHETICAL PURCHASE

Single Family Home

POTENTIAL RENT:	MONTHLY	ANNUALLY
	$1,200.00	$14,400.00
Vacancy Reserve 5%:	-$60.00	-$720.00
Repair Reserve 10%:	-$120.00	-$1,440.00
Insurance:	-$75.00	-$900.00
Property Taxes:	-$150.00	-$1,800.00
Interest Expense:	$0.00	$0.00
Water:	$0.00	$0.00
Trash/$18 Per Unit:	$0.00	$0.00
Mowing/Average Over 12 Months:	$0.00	$0.00
Professional Management 10%	-$120.00	-$1,440.00
TOTAL EXPENSES:	**-$525.00**	**-$6,300.00**
NET PROFIT:	**$675.00**	**$8,100.00**
Estimated Appreciation:		3.00%
VALUE BASED ON AN ROI OF 6%:		**$135,000.00**
VALUE BASED ON AN ROI OF 8%:		**$101,250.00**
VALUE BASED ON AN ROI OF 10%:		**$81,000.00**

This hypothetical Cincinnati, Ohio property should make at least $8,100.00 a year. In addition, Zillow.com reports that the property is forecasted to appreciate 3% this year. You decide based on the strength of the market that an annual operating return of 8% would be acceptable. Based on these facts, you value the property at $101,250.

You anticipate that your total return at this price will be 11%. (8% ROI plus 3% appreciation equals 11%.) There may also be significant income tax savings to be captured depending on your personal financial situation. You do not wish to pay a premium for the expected appreciation, so the hoped for 3% annual increase in the value of the property will be a bonus to you. Here is the math:

$8,100.00 annual return/buy the required ROI of 8% = $101,250.00.

You now know that the maximum you should pay for the property is $91,250. ($101,250 less the $10,000 you are going to put into the property for cosmetic updates immediately after purchase.) You decide to open negotiations at $80,000. Regardless of where the negotiations end up, you are in a powerful position because you are working with hard facts. You can make an informed decision to either move forward with the best deal you can make, or wait for the next opportunity to come along.

The Cost of Financing a Single Family Home

I am going to use a house that I own in Springfield to illustrate the cost and benefits of financing a purchase. Here is the return on investment analysis.

CASE STUDY #5
MURRAY STREET
AS CASH PURCHASE

Single Family Home

PURCHASE PRICE:		$25,000.00
Rehab:		$0.00
TOTAL INVESTMENT:		**$25,000.00**

POTENTIAL RENT:	MONTHLY	ANNUALLY
Unit 1:	$550.00	$6,600.00
Unit 2::	$0.00	$0.00
TOTAL:	**$550.00**	**$6,600.00**
Vacancy Reserve 10%:	-$55.00	-$660.00
Repair Reserve 20%:	-$110.00	-$1,320.00
Insurance:	-$40.00	-$480.00
Property Taxes:	-$48.00	-$576.00
Interest Expense:	$0.00	$0.00
Water:	$0.00	$0.00
Trash/$18 Per Unit:	$0.00	$0.00
Mowing/Average Over 12 Months:	$0.00	$0.00
Professional Management 10%	-$55.00	-$660.00
TOTAL EXPENSES:	**-$308.00**	**-$3,696.00**
NET PROFIT:	**$242.00**	**$2,904.00**
Estimated Appreciation:		0.00%
ANNUAL ROI:		**11.67%**

My ability to buy this house via land contract was the main reason I compromised on my 15% default goal. I paid $25,000 and it had a tenant in place at closing. I agreed to a $2,500 down payment and a mortgage of $22,500 at 10% over 10 years. This meant a monthly principle and interest payment of $296.

From a profitability perspective, the interest I pay becomes an expense and negatively impacts my return. As you can see below, my ROI drops from 12.10% to 6.38% with the added interest expense factored in. To simplify this example, I am averaging the total amount of interest I will pay over the ten year period. In reality, the interest peaks during the first year and steadily declines over the remaining term until the last few payments are almost all principle. (Bankrate.com has a great mortgage payment calculator that allows you to print amortization schedules based on whatever parameters you choose.)

CASE STUDY #6
MURRAY STREET
WITH INTEREST EXPENSE

Single Family Home

PURCHASE PRICE:		$25,000.00
Rehab:		$0.00
TOTAL INVESTMENT:		$25,000.00

POTENTIAL RENT:	**MONTHLY**	**ANNUALLY**
Unit 1:	$550.00	$6,600.00
Unit 2::	$0.00	$0.00
TOTAL:	$550.00	$6,600.00

Vacancy Reserve 10%:	-$55.00	-$660.00
Repair Reserve 20%:	-$110.00	-$1,320.00
Insurance:	-$40.00	-$480.00
Property Taxes:	-$48.00	-$576.00
Interest Expense/Average over 7 Year Term:	-$109.00	-$1,308.00
Water:	$0.00	$0.00
Trash/$18 Per Unit:	$0.00	$0.00
Mowing/Average Over 12 Months:	$0.00	$0.00
Professional Management 10%	-$55.00	-$660.00
TOTAL EXPENSES:	-$417.00	-$5,004.00

NET PROFIT:	$133.00	$1,596.00
Estimated Appreciation:		0.00%

ANNUAL ROI:	6.38%

Total interest over the life of the mortgage is $13,031.35/120 months = **$108.59 per month.**

Now let's look at how having a mortgage on this property affects my cash flow. Financing negatively impacts my cash flow because I have to pay the total amortized payment of $296 a month out of my gross income. The interest portion of each payment over the term of the seven year loan is expensed, while the principle portion of each payment is part of my profit.

CASE STUDY #7
MURRAY STREET
CASH FLOW ANALYSIS

Single Family Home

PURCHASE PRICE:		$24,000.00
Rehab:		$0.00
TOTAL INVESTMENT:		**$24,000.00**

POTENTIAL RENT:	MONTHLY	ANNUALLY
Unit 1:	$550.00	$6,600.00
Unit 2::	$0.00	$0.00
TOTAL:	**$550.00**	**$6,600.00**
Vacancy Reserve 10%:	-$55.00	-$660.00
Repair Reserve 20%:	-$110.00	-$1,320.00
Insurance:	-$40.00	-$480.00
Property Taxes:	-$48.00	-$576.00
Total Monthly Mortgage Payment, Principle and Interest:	-$296.00	-$3,552.00
Water:	$0.00	$0.00
Trash/$18 Per Unit:	$0.00	$0.00
Mowing/Average Over 12 Months:	$0.00	$0.00
Professional Management 10%	-$55.00	-$660.00
TOTAL EXPENSES:	**-$604.00**	**-$7,248.00**
FREE CASH FLOW UNTIL MORTGAGE IS PAID OFF:	**-$54.00**	**-$648.00**
Estimated Appreciation:		0.00%

As you can see, I am planning to be upside down from a cash flow perspective as much as $648 a year on this property. I am comfortable with this possible worst case outcome, but so far I have had no vacancies and my repair expenses have been minimal. Consequently I am breaking even on this property and have yet to put any additional cash towards it to keep it afloat.

Financing this property made perfect sense for me. I was able to buy a house I did not have the cash for, and at the end of a ten years I will own it out right. I structured the deal so that if I do find myself in a negative cash flow position, my exposure is limited. There is also room to raise the rent another $50 to $75 a month after this tenant moves out, and in all likelihood I will pay the mortgage off early. In my opinion this is how an investor should utilize financing.

The Cost of Financing a Side By Side Double

Here is another property that I financed.

CASE STUDY #8
CENTER STREET
AS CASH PURCHASE

Side By Side Double

PURCHASE PRICE:		$20,000.00
Rehab:		$43,125.00
TOTAL INVESTMENT:		**$63,125.00**

POTENTIAL RENT:	MONTHLY	ANNUALLY
Unit 1:	$550.00	$6,600.00
Unit 2::	$550.00	$6,600.00
TOTAL:	**$1,100.00**	**$13,200.00**
Vacancy Reserve 10%:	-$110.00	-$1,320.00
Repair Reserve 20%:	-$220.00	-$2,640.00
Insurance:	-$60.00	-$720.00
Property Taxes:	-$26.00	-$312.00
Interest Expense:	$0.00	$0.00
Water:	-$35.00	-$420.00
Trash/$18 Per Unit:	-$36.00	-$432.00
Mowing/Average Over 12 Months:	-$35.00	$420.00
Professional Management 10%	-$110.00	-$1,320.00
TOTAL EXPENSES:	**-$632.00**	**-$7,584.00**
NET PROFIT:	**$468.00**	**$5,616.00**
Estimated Appreciation:		0.00%
ANNUAL ROI:		**8.90%**

This property is comparatively superior to most of the other properties I own. It is also in a neighborhood that has been easy for us to rent in. I initially bought the house for $20,000 on a 7-year land contract and sat on it for almost 3 years before rehabbing it. The house had new vinyl siding, a new roof and all new windows, but it was just bare studs inside. It cost me an additional $43,125 to make it habitable over the course of a year.

I did over-improve this property to some degree, but I did a quality job and I expect it to outperform my portfolio over the long term. By the time I started the project I had opened a line of credit at a local bank secured by a couple of properties I owned free and clear. I used the line of credit to rehab the property. Once it was completed, I financed the property with a $33,800, 15-year mortgage at 5% interest. I used the proceeds to pay down the line of credit.

Here are the numbers including the average monthly interest expense. Like with the Murray Street property, I averaged the total amount of interest I will pay over the 15 year/180 month term of the mortgage. In reality, the interest peaks during the first year and steadily declines over the remaining term until the last few payments are almost all principle.

CASE STUDY #9
CENTER STREET WITH INTEREST EXPENSE

Side By Side Double

PURCHASE PRICE:		$20,000.00
Rehab:		$43,125.00
TOTAL INVESTMENT:		$63,125.00

POTENTIAL RENT:	**MONTHLY**	**ANNUALLY**
Unit 1:	$550.00	$6,600.00
Unit 2::	$550.00	$6,600.00
TOTAL:	**$1,100.00**	**$13,200.00**
Vacancy Reserve 10%:	-$110.00	-$1,320.00
Repair Reserve 20%:	-$220.00	-$2,640.00
Insurance:	-$60.00	-$720.00
Property Taxes:	-$26.00	-$312.00
Interest Expense/Average over 15 Year Term:	-$79.51	-$954.12
Water:	-$35.00	-$420.00
Trash/$18 Per Unit:	-$36.00	-$432.00
Mowing/Average Over 12 Months:	-$35.00	$420.00
Professional Management 10%	-$110.00	-$1,320.00
TOTAL EXPENSES:	**-$711.00**	**-$8,538.12**
NET PROFIT:	**$388.49**	**$4,661.88**
Estimated Appreciation:		0.00%
ANNUAL ROI:		**7.39%**

Total interest over the life of the mortgage is $14,311.88/180 months = **$79.51 per month.**

The cash flow analysis for this property shows that worst case, I should have positive cashflow of approximately $200 per month.

CASE STUDY #10
CENTER STREET
CASH FLOW ANALYSIS

Side By Side Double

PURCHASE PRICE:		$20,000.00
Rehab:		$43,125.00
TOTAL INVESTMENT:		$63,125.00

POTENTIAL RENT:	**MONTHLY**	**ANNUALLY**
Unit 1:	$550.00	$6,600.00
Unit 2::	$550.00	$6,600.00
TOTAL:	**$1,100.00**	**$13,200.00**
Vacancy Reserve 10%:	-$110.00	-$1,320.00
Repair Reserve 20%:	-$220.00	-$2,640.00
Insurance:	-$60.00	-$720.00
Property Taxes:	-$26.00	-$312.00
Total Monthly Mortgage Payment, Principle and Interest:	-$267.08	-$3,204.96
Water:	-$35.00	-$420.00
Trash/$18 Per Unit:	-$36.00	-$432.00
Mowing/Average Over 12 Months:	-$35.00	$420.00
Professional Management 10%	-$110.00	-$1.320.00
TOTAL EXPENSES:	**-$899.08**	**-$10,788.96**
FREE CASH FLOW UNTIL MORTGAGE IS PAID OF:	**$200.92**	**$2,411.04**
Estimated Appreciation:		0.00%

Cash on Cash Return

Another way to evaluate this property is to look at its 'cash on cash' return. I have roughly $29,325 of my own money in this deal. The bank started with $33,800. My net profit after interest expense is projected to be $4,661.88 annually (See Case Study #9). Taking the net profit of $4661.88 and dividing it by the $29,325 I have in the deal, equals a cash on cash return of 15.9%. I really like owning this property.

Avoiding Bankruptcy

Financing to term is the ONLY financing that makes sense. Financing to term means your lender is going to hold the note for the entire amortization period. Many loans are amortized over say twenty years, but they have a balloon payment due in say 10 years. This means you have to either pay off the balance of the loan or be in a position to extend the loan or refinance it at the ten-year mark. I do not want have to count on being able to do that.

Taking a mortgage that results in negative cash flow is a sure path to bankruptcy. Lots of people will teach you how to borrow money, not one of them will teach you how to pay it back.
Real estate is not a liquid investment. You can't write a check against it, and you can't cash it out at a moment's notice like a stock or bond. Even selling a house at a fire sale price for cash takes a few days to close. Debt can ruin you if you don't control it and yourself.

And One More Thing - Get a Good Accountant

The tax benefits of investing in real estate are many. Personal tax strategy is well beyond the scope of this book and my personal expertise. What I can tell you is that you must find an accountant that understands real estate investing. Best case—they should own investment property themselves, or at a minimum have an extensive client base of investors.

I am on my fourth accountant in 16 years. I can tell you from personal experience that you can ask four different accountants the same question and get four different answers. I hate to think of the tax I overpaid in various years, but I am grateful to have finally found a professional that understands my situation. Ask your business associates, friends and advisors for referrals. Take your time and do your homework. Your accountant can be major resource and aid to your profitability, or they can cost you a lot of money.

Conclusion

My main goal for this section of the book is to help you avoid falling into the Magical Thinking trap. I want you to buy your house right and plan for all of the eventualities that can affect your profitability both good and bad. It is far easier to lose money investing in real estate than it is to make it. I know this from personal experience. I hope this chapter helps you avoid the same mistakes I made. Part 5:

WHAT HAS TO HAPPEN FOR HOUSING PRICES TO STABILIZE?—FEBRUARY 2009

I am no economist but from what I see on a day-to-day basis in my profession, and in most of what I read, foreclosure filings must stabilize before housing prices will end their free-fall. Further complicating matters, of course, is the overall employment situation. Rising incomes drive home sales, and lost jobs drive up foreclosure filings. In a healthy housing market, the most important variable in home prices is personal income. It is a complicated equation, but a great situation for investors with access to cash and a 3-10 year time horizon in which to hold properties.

Banks normally do one of two things in a default situation. They either foreclose, or work with the borrower to help them stay in their home. In the past, almost everyone wanted to stay in their homes. Today's situation is different because as home values fall, a greater number of borrowers have no desire to stay in a home that is worth so much less than the amount owed on it. Many owner-occupants—and many investors—are simply walking away from their properties. They want to give their properties back to the banks. In some cases, borrowers with the ability to make their payments are walking away as well.

One solution to the problem has been to establish moratoriums on foreclosures. Several institutions simply halted foreclosure filings during the fourth quarter of 2008. It is unclear whether this will ultimately help solve the problem or simply delay the inevitable. I am of the opinion that it will delay the inevitable for most borrowers. However, anything that slows the deluge of vacant and distressed properties to market is a positive for home values in the near term.

Also of note, Fannie Mae and Freddie Mac are no longer evicting tenants who wish to stay in their properties. They can stay in the properties as long as they pay their rent. This is a new approach to delaying placing additional housing stock on the market.

The Streamlined Mortgage Plan introduced by HOPE NOW in late 2008 is another initiative that is gaining traction among lenders. HOPE NOW is an alliance of counselors, mortgage market participants, and mortgage servicers that is working to help as many homeowners as possible avoid foreclosure and stay in their homes. For details of the streamlined modification plan visit www.hopenow.com .

In a recent issue of Default Servicing News magazine (www.dsnews.com) Ed Delgado, SVP of Mortgage Industry Relations and Default Information Analytics at Wells Fargo, wrote the following in support of the Streamlined Mortgage Plan and his company's plans to put it into practice:

"The new modification process starts when we notify customers who are likely to be eligible and ask them to call us. They must provide proof of income, a signed hardship letter that demonstrates a change in their financial situation, and a signed affidavit confirming that their default was unavoidable due to unforeseen circumstances."

Here is a summary of their process:

- Upon receipt of the hardship letter and affidavit, Wells Fargo will extend the loan term to 40 years and reduce the interest rate to achieve a mortgage debt to income ratio of 38%. The interest rate reduction has a floor of 3%.

- If further modification is required to get to a mortgage debt to income ratio of 38%, a portion of the loan principle may be set aside. No interest is attached to the set aside portion of principle but the customer will have to make a balloon payment at the point the loan is paid off. This is allowed if the new principle is not less than the current value of the property

- In the short term the customer must show that they can make the payments for three months before the modification is officially put in place.

This is aggressive action and a model that most large banks are likely to follow. However, it will delay the inevitable if prices do not stabilize almost immediately and begin to rise again in the near term. Obviously, these actions will not help everybody, but if they help even a fraction of borrowers keep their properties it will slow the number of distressed properties coming to market.

Congress and President Obama are floating several ideas to stimulate home buying. There is an assumption that there are buyers out there sitting on the sidelines waiting for mortgage rates to drop and or asking prices to drop further. These people need to be pushed off the fence. Among these ideas is a $15,000 tax credit to any buyer who buys a new personal residence. This is a huge step from the current policy of offer a $7,500 tax credit to first time buyers that must be paid back over time.

Tax credits to home buyers are great but they amount to no more than a government subsidy to the home building industry. In many parts of the country we still have too much housing stock on hand and not enough qualified buyers with stable good paying jobs. Don't get me wrong, I support initiatives like these but we need to be realistic about the current situation and understand that this will not be a magic bullet.

Regardless of the efficacy of government and private efforts to solve the problem, the bottom line is many borrowers need to get out of their current situation and into one that they can afford. The best solution will be one that acknowledges a buyer's true economic abilities and offers an appropriate response.

In the same issue of Default Servicing News referenced above, Robert J. Hopp, an attorney with Robert J. Hopp and Associates wrote:

"...perhaps the best program to help struggling borrowers going into 2009 would be to critically look at the borrower's ability to meet their monthly obligations and assist them in adjusting their finances accordingly. In some cases, this may mean that homeowners need to become renters. Although this approach may not curtail foreclosures, the return to modest borrower spending and focusing on that old lost habit of saving will allow us to start rebuilding the housing market with strong borrowers resilient to the next rainy day that is sure to come."

Without a doubt, that is the most rational response the current situation I have heard to date – though wishful thinking I'm afraid.

While all of the above initiatives are better than nothing, 2009 and 2010 will be tough years for housing prices. By some estimates there are still trillions of dollars in defaults to come as resets on option-ARM loan products begin occur this year and next on loans written in 2004 and 2005 – the peak of the housing bubble. The silver lining of course is that 2009 and 2010 will offer incredible opportunities for real estate investors. We at My Real Estate Life™ are here to help you navigate the turbulent times and identify the opportunities that will pay off in the long run. These are indeed interesting times we live in.

WE STILL HAVE A WAY TO GO— JUNE 2009

Since the real estate downturn began four years ago this month, I have often wondered what the bottom would look like, and if we would recognize it when it came. Like any macro-economic occurrence, we may only recognize the shift in hindsight. I am convinced that while the worst may be over, unemployment alone will result in more distressed home sales over the next couple of years.

Here is why I think we still have a way to go:

- Interest rates are ticking up and new fees are being charged.
- The HVCC or Home Valuation Code of Conduct is kicking in.
- Prime fixed-rate mortgage default rates are trending up.
- Re-defaults are rising after workout plans fail.
- Foreclosure moratoriums expired in March.
- Case-Shiller Home Price Index continues to show a decline in home values.

Some signs we are closer to the bottom than we were 30 days ago:

- The Obama Administration is coming out with a standardized short sale process.
- High end home sales continue to crash and refinancing jumbo mortgages is next to impossible.
- The $8,000 first time buyer tax credit is working – and may be increased by the end of the year.

On the interest rate front, we were seeing sub 5% 30 year fixed rates for most of this year. Rates are as high as 5.75% now. In addition Fannie and Freddie are adding on some new fees to their mix(es). According to the Los Angeles Times in an April 18, 2009 article, "borrowers are being hit with extra fees of 3% to 5% because of the type of property they want to buy or refinance, their credit scores, or the size of their down payment."

Some major lenders who sell loans to Freddie and Fannie are tightening their underwriting standards beyond what Freddie and Fannie require. New credit score minimums and down payment requirements are going up. Financing condominiums is getting both harder and more expensive across the board further depressing markets like south Florida.

On the appraisal front, Fannie and Freddie are now requiring a 'market condition' report adding $45 to $50 to the cost of an appraisal. The Home Valuation Code of Conduct is posing new hurdles as well. Mortgage brokers can no longer order appraisals directly but must utilize third party appraisal management companies. While there are clearly good reasons for this approach, the net result is added cost. There is also the issue of appraisers now working in markets they are unfamiliar with affecting the accuracy of evaluations.

Diana Olick of CNBC.com 'Realty Check' reported on May 28th that prime mortgages have "finally leapfrogged those nasty subprimes to take the lead in the race to foreclosure." Almost half of the increase in foreclosures in the first quarter of 2009 were due to prime mortgages. Many of these borrowers are educated professionals adversely impacted by the current job market. However, others simply were living beyond their means and exhausted their savings and maxed out their credit cards. Loan modifications will not help these people ultimately bringing new inventory to market.

What about the highly publicized work out plans sponsored by Hope Now and others? Many borrowers are defaulting on loans that have already been modified. For many if not most, loan modifications and the foreclosure moratoriums instituted in late 2008 that expired in March 2009, simply delayed the inevitable. In addition, it is estimated that 40% of homes in foreclosure are already vacant with no hope of a loan modification changing the outcome. Many borrowers who are upside down on their mortgages continue to walk away.

Finally, and strictly by the numbers, the housing bust continues. According to the latest Case-Shiller numbers, home prices are off 36% from their peak in 2006. (Where we are in Ohio, our peak was June 2005.) Regionally of course there are disparities. The boom areas like Florida, Nevada and California are way off compared to Texas for instance.

Signs of a Bottom?

All of the above in my opinion mean extended opportunities for real estate investors – but for how long? Here are three points that may signal that we are approaching a floor on what we can buy houses for, but a real upswing in what we will be able to sell them for going forward.

On May 14th the Obama administration announced incentives and standardized procedures for short sale under the Foreclosure Alternatives Program. Why is this news and why does it point to a bottom? To date, banks have been unwilling or unable to complete short sales in a timely manner resulting in more REO inventory hitting the market. This could tighten up inventory over time resulting in higher prices for distressed property.

In addition, the Making Home Affordable plan announced in April includes provisions for including second mortgages in loan modification programs. While, the default rates on previously modified loans are running as high as 46%, this common sense approach to helping people who want to stay in their homes do so, makes sense to me. Again, this could reduce the number of distressed properties coming on the market over time.

High end home sale deterioration means greater demand for lower to mid-priced housing stock where most investors we work with specialize. It is unclear where the demand will come from in the future for these 'McMansion' type properties, located well beyond urban centers of commerce – especially if they cannot be financed. Regardless of what happens to these neighborhoods, some of these property owners will walk away voluntarily or be forced through foreclosure to find more affordable housing closer to where they work.

Finally, the first time buyer tax credit is working and lobbyists from many corners are pushing to extend the credit beyond the December 2009 deadline. In addition, there are calls to double the size of the credit and make it available to all buyers. Two stats should be of note to investors. One, close to 70% of all homes sales this year have involved distressed properties. Two, fully 50% of all purchases in the last 90 days have been made by first time home buyers. This trend will continue in my opinion into 2010. This type of demand will ultimately absorb existing inventory and improve the supply and demand ratio.

So short term, six to nine months we will see a tsunami of new REO inventory based on 2008/2009 foreclosure moratorium expirations, and the effect of job losses on prime borrowers. Simultaneously however, we will see demand for affordable housing rise, and government policies stimulate the housing market. We should see values begin to rise in 2010 and 2011 as demand begins to outpace supply.

Obviously, there is enough turmoil in the market to ensure opportunities for investors will remain for the foreseeable future. On the other hand, there is reason to believe wholesale and REO prices will begin to moderate sooner rather than later. If you have been waiting on the sidelines for the market to bottom, it may be time to go back to work.

What are you seeing where you are? What are your predictions for your market or the country as a whole? We want to hear from you at www.MyRealEstateLifeOnline.com.

WHERE MOST PEOPLE GET HURT AND WHY
MAINTENANCE AND REPAIRS

PART 5: WHERE MOST PEOPLE GET HURT AND WHY - MAINTENANCE AND REPAIRS

In all of the years we have been doing this, nothing has caused me, my clients and our management team more heartache and consternation than repairs, maintenance, and rehabs. I resisted doing rehabs for our clients for a long time. This was because of the difficulty I had getting projects done for myself within the budget I had in mind. I would explicitly tell people that we are a management firm not a construction firm.

We preferred that our clients bring us finished properties. We were happy to handle ongoing maintenance with our employees in occupied properties, but rehabs were another story. After much reflection, I came to the realization that, if we could offer construction management services to our clients, we could probably double or triple our business. In 2012, we decided to make initial rehabbing and completing large 'turn' projects between tenants a central pillar of our value proposition.

After my 'Aha' moment, we made plans to hold a Contractor Lunch and Information Session at our office in Springfield. We asked everyone we knew to recommend who we should invite. We ended up with over thirty people attending. Almost all of our guests were independent contractors who were already doing rehab work either full or part-time.

Our agenda focused on the following:

- Background about our company.
- How many properties we managed and hoped to manage in the future.
- The number of rehabs and turn projects we needed help with each month.
- What we expected from our contractor partners.

- What our contractor partners should expect from us.
- What their bids and estimates needed to include.
- How and when they would be paid.

Quoting Labor and Materials

Our policy is to obtain two bids for each project. Each contractor is to quote labor and estimate materials separately. This gives us more control over the project. Even though we will generally supply the materials, the estimate supplied by the contractor gives the owner an idea of the total cost of the project before committing to going forward.

Some of our larger clients have their own Lowe's or Home Depot contractor accounts and pay for the materials based on the contractor's shopping list. For other smaller projects and repairs in occupied units, our employees purchase materials on our Lowe's or Home Depot account, and we bill back the owner during the next rent cycle. This way there is no question about the cost of materials incurred by our owners. We have all of the receipts.

We pride ourselves on not marking up the cost of projects we manage for our owners. We see getting the properties ready for rent as part of the service we provide. Many property management companies charge a surcharge or obtain 'rebates' from the contractors they send work to. In my experience, this is a common reason investors lose confidence in their management company and decide to make a change. We have never done that and never will.

Having said that, there is one place where we charge our owners an administrative fee and it is outlined quite clearly in our management agreement. (See Part 7 - The Basics of Management – How We Do It.) The last sentence in paragraph six states "Materials purchased on our accounts are billed at 110% of purchase price and tax to cover clerical and billing costs." As you can imagine, there are months when there are literally hundreds of entries on our monthly statement that must be assigned to different owners and their properties.

Once we obtain a quote or quotes for a project, our property manager reviews them and scans and emails them to the owner for approval. Again, the actual cost of labor and materials as quoted by the contractor is the expense our owners incur. This policy applies to lawn mowing and snow removal contractors as well as third party service providers like licensed plumber's and electricians. Our owners make the final decision as what work is going to be done and who is going to do it.

We also ask the contractor to provide a timeline for completion. While there are times when a project will start and finish earlier than expected, there are more times when the project takes longer than we think it should. While we never allow an open-ended time line for a project, the less expensive contractors tend to take longer to finish the job. There is a direct correlation in our experience between the cost of labor and how long it will take. It is a factor the owner and the property manager have to consider before automatically awarding a job to the contractor with the lowest bid.

If the contractor is supplying materials for a project, they will want a material check before starting work. Larger projects may warrant interim labor payments at predetermined completion milestones. In these situations we ask our owners to keep money for the project in our Property Management Trust Account. Once a contractor meets a milestone or completes the project, the property manager inspects the project and if all is well, releases the owner's funds for payment.

Our Maintenance Team

In addition to the cadre of independent contractors who do initial rehabs and between-tenant turns for our owners, we have a team of qualified maintenance people on our payroll. Being employees, they are covered by our general liability and worker's compensation insurance policies. As a liability mitigation measure, we will only allow our employees to do work within tenant occupied units. We cannot send people we do not know into tenants' homes.

Our senior maintenance team members can do most HVAC, plumbing and minor electrical work. They have decades of experience between them and have been with us for several years. Consequently, they are paid well. As I write this in September of 2016, we bill our owners back for maintenance and repairs at $29.00 per hour for business hours and $42.80 per hour for after-hours and weekend work. These costs are also outlined in paragraph six of our sample management agreement in Part 7 of this book.

Our maintenance team members supply their own tools and transportation, and we pay them mileage and travel time between jobs in fifteen minute increments. These costs are passed along to our owners as well. The hourly cost of our employees is not insignificant. However, our owners have found over the years that having our people handle an HVAC emergency or a broken pipe situation in the dead of winter is far less expensive than hiring a third party contractor to do the same work – even at after-hours rates.

Maintenance Answering Service

Our tenant service standard is to complete routine requests within 72 hours and to stay in touch with the tenant throughout the process. There is nothing more frustrating for a tenant than having something broken in their home and not be able to get it fixed. Our property management software vendor (Appfolio) provides us with a 24 hour answering service for maintenance requests from our tenants. If a tenant has an emergency situation or a routine request, they call an 800 number and speak to a live person. Here is the description of the service from the Appfolio website, www.Appfolio.com.

MANAGE ALL WORK ORDERS FOR A PROJECT IN ONE SERVICE REQUEST.

All in One Maintenance Management

The AppFolio Service Request feature enables easy maintenance management for a project, from a single work order to multiple work orders with multiple vendors, all together in one service request. You have the flexibility to handle any size project you need to get done.

You can set the priority as urgent, normal or low to clearly define and organize your Service Requests projects. Add owner contact information, vendor instructions and define maintenance roles. In addition, Service Requests Management allows you to track time spent on the job by your in-house maintenance staff all in one property management work order software.

Property maintenance management becomes much easier with AppFolio Service Requests. You can also configure standard, recurring Service Request work orders for typical move-in/move-out jobs as well as standard monthly or annual maintenance tasks.

Easily Communicate Service Requests

Using Appfolio's paperless Service Request feature to communicate with vendors allows you to respond to and solve property maintenance issues much faster. Your residents will appreciate how quickly you address and fix property issues using effective maintenance management, and you can keep owners aware of your progress with email updates and copies of work orders.

Fully Integrated Work Order Management

Service Requests are fully integrated with accounting and leasing functionality in AppFolio property management software. Receive maintenance management requests from the tenant portal, track time spent on the job, easily create bills, and create an AppFolio Service Request on the fly when you're inspecting a property through the Mobile Inspections feature in AppFolio.

The system allows us to designate what is considered an emergency and who is to be contacted to do the work for each unit under management. If an owner is doing his or her own maintenance, the service will contact the owner directly. All maintenance requests are documented on our management portal and on the Appfolio mobile tablet application. Our maintenance team members each carry an Android tablet running the Appfolio system.

WHAT CONTRACTORS CAN EXPECT WHEN THEY WORK WITH ROOST™

We strive to treat the independent contractors we hire as if they were internal team members on our payroll. They require and deserve the same leadership commitment as an employee. Our goal is to attract and retain the finest rehab partners we can. Here is what our contractors can expect form us:

Top 10 Reasons to Work with ROOST Real Estate Co.

1. FAST/CONSISTENT Payment
Checks for draws and reimbursements are scheduled for deliver every Friday by noon

2. Lock Boxes on Every Property
No more waiting for someone to show up to unlock the door so you can begin

3. Easy Process
We define project scope, you complete project, we create punch list, you complete punch list items, we review punch list, you receive payment same day.

4. Vacant Homes
No home-owner living in the house means no moving furniture, no covering up couches to paint, no taping off TV sets to prevent damage, no moving fragile decorations

5. Flexible Working Hours
Because our homes are vacant, you can work anytime you want. (Just don't keep our neighbors up with loud banging or running saws or hammering or whatever! We love our neighbors

6. Consistent Income
We rehab up to a dozen houses a month and we're always looking for quality contractors and sub-contractors.

7. Great Owners
Honest. Fair. Realistic. Straightforward.

8. No Committees, No Pointless Meetings, No Bureaucracy
Decision are made quickly and efficiently.

9. Same Style, Same Colors, Same Materials, and Same Fixtures
We always use the same materials, paints, fixtures, etc. in each of our houses so our contractors don't have to guess what type of light fixtures to buy or color to paint or windows to order.

10. Quality Product
We want all of our homes to look much the same. We want a prospective buyer to walk into our house and say, "This is a ROOST House"

WHAT WE EXPECT FROM OUR CONTRACTOR PARTNERS

What Success with ROOST Real Estate Co. Looks Like

The End Result
Our expectations for the end results our contractor teams produce are no different than what any other client expects. We expect our projects to be finished on time, within budget and to our specifications for quality.

On Time
Every project is unique in some way. Prior to starting a project for an owner we will sit down with you and discuss what will make the property a successful investment and get your input on how long it will take to complete. Once we all understand the scope of the project we will set a deadline for completion.

On Budget
Again, every project is unique, but our homes are all the same in terms of the type, style and color of materials used. This helps us accurately estimate costs together. Yes, unexpected things can come up during a project, but as a rule, our contractors come in on budget. Planning, involving the entire team, accurate estimates, and sticking to the plan are the keys to making the numbers.

On Standard
Every home we rehab for a client needs to be a ROOST™ Way home. We may miss a budget or a deadline from time to time but we NEVER put an inferior product on the market. On standard means that on turnover day, the house is done. We are not talking about "substantial completion". It is finished and ready for market.

Stay Focused on the Tenant

We have seen investors become very product-focused when embarking on a new purchase and rehab project. The worst thing an investor can do is lose sight of what it takes to attract tenants in a competitive market. We believe product focus has to be balanced with a client-focused attitude.

Product-focused investors can become wrapped up in potential returns versus what the market or a specific property can and will return. It is easy to cut corners here and there when preparing a home for rent and suddenly find oneself with a house that looks great on paper, but is not appealing to an actual buyer or tenant when compared to others on the street.

The client-focused attitude has to be top of mind during the planning and purchase process so that any costs associated with finishing a competitive product are incorporated up front. Having to incur unforeseen costs at the end to make a property competitive in the marketplace will negatively impact your return on investment. For planning purposes it is prudent to add 20% to whatever you think the final cost of a project will be.

Preparing a Home for a New Tenant

At a minimum, every unit we manage, regardless of the value of the investment, has to be safe, clean, and secure with all mechanical systems in working order. We also recommend that the property be upgraded to the neighborhood standard - but no more. We want to offer the best value in the neighborhood, but if we can rent a house for less than the competition and still get a fair return, everybody wins.

Most of the mistakes I made early in my investing career involved over-improving properties. In effect, improving them beyond the neighborhood standard. However, there were times when I was just wrong about how much things really cost. While it is natural to want to negotiate with a contractor on his or her labor bid, it is helpful to keep in mind the costs they hopefully considered before submitting their bed.

A reputable contractor with an established work history is going to have some overhead. This overhead may include transportation costs, insurance, local licenses, and tools to name a few. A low bid that does not include these considerations can end up costing you money and or time down the road. Remember, we have eliminated the possibility of 'slush' in a bid by separating labor costs from material costs. We are only paying for the actual cost of materials and no more. A labor quote that seems too good to be true probably is.

Consider These Suggestions When Renovating a Home to Rent

Here are a few items other investors may not do:

- Replace the toilet(s) or at least the seat. Use the larger units found in new homes.

- Install air conditioning

- Make as many things handicap accessible possible. (Bathtub grab bars, for instance.)

- Dishwashers are appreciated – stick with a very basic unit.

- Install garage door openers. Remotes can be replaced inexpensively.
- Exterior lighting – make sure what is there works.
- If there is a partial fence, consider completing it and/or installing gates that can be secured if they are missing.
- Install storm doors front and rear.
- Washer and dryer hookups are imperative.
- Keep the grass mowed and trimmed. Pull old bushes out and add mulch and maintenance free foundation plantings.
- Install a new mailbox and house numbers.
- In Ohio, vinyl replacement windows are a big selling point and we are continually amazed at how many investors skip this step in an effort to save money. Check Lowe's and Home Depot prices against local sources.
- Paint the basement walls and the basement floor, including the stairs leading to the basement. This goes a long way towards showing the care you took with the rehab.
- Clean and touch-up paint furnace and water heater.

It often is the little things that help the most.

Conclusion

My goal here is to get you thinking about all of the things that go into rehabs, repairs, and the ongoing maintenance of investment properties. I have seen more people get into financial trouble because of either overpaying for services or underestimating what these services really cost. Successfully taking care of tenant emergencies and maintenance concerns in a timely manner will reduce your tenant turnover and improve your occupancy rates as well. In my blog post below from 2009, I highlighted in more detail why this part of the business can be so frustrating for so many investors.

CONTRACTOR OVERHEAD AND THE PERILS OF THE LOWEST BID - MARCH 2009

Brad and I have always had the philosophy that we both need to do what we do best, and hire out the rest. This philosophy has served us well, but it means that we hire out all aspects of the rehab process. We have been disappointed at the end of many of our projects because we did not make as much money as we thought we would when we bought the property.

Many of our problems stemmed from hiring unqualified individuals either from a technical standpoint, a business standpoint, or both. Most of our problems however were a result of the disconnect between what we believed rehab and construction services should cost, versus what a reputable contractor has to charge to make a fair and decent living.

Obtaining a Contractor's License

In Ohio—and we presume in other states as well—there are no standards and no licensing requirements for general contractors. Proof of general liability insurance, workers compensation insurance, a $10,000 bond and $300 is all it takes to obtain a local license. There is no professional or business training required. I think this explains why such a high percentage of contractors fail, and fail quickly. Remodeling is a tough business even for those who are experienced and the best in the field.

What Construction Services Actually Cost

Even now when we walk through houses we catch ourselves estimating repairs based on what we think they should cost, instead of thinking through what they actually do cost us. Many investors think they are going to get a job done for a certain amount of money by sheer force of will. Some people tarnish their reputations by bullying contractors to do their bidding and are constantly going through new people. We have seen this approach work, but it is not for us.

Cost and Mark-Up

The major mistakes contractors make when bidding a project include the obvious and not so obvious. One, there is the actual cost of hiring someone to do the work. Sounds easy, but by how much should the contractor markup that work? If the contractor is doing some or most of the physical labor, how much is he going to pay himself? Is he charging enough to cover his or her personal obligations? If well into the job he realizes he is not charging you enough to pay his bills, rest assured he will be distracted from the work at hand.

Second, there is the question of covering their overhead. Even the guy who works out of his house or truck has overhead. Overhead can add 20% to 40% to actual job costs. Overhead items any contractor must consider include at least some of the following:

- Insurance
- Taxes
- Workmen's Compensation Insurance
- Interest expense
- Tools and equipment
- Bad Debt
- Licensing and fees
- Accounting and bookkeeping
- Legal Fees
- Education and training
- Association Fees

- Vehicles
- Car Insurance
- Service and call backs
- Telephone
- Internet access
- Office expense
- Office Supplies
- Staff Expense
- Advertising
- Sales and Marketing

In essence, any and all of the expenses any business owner has.

If it is clear that if you have a job quote that cannot possibly take into account reasonable and customary expenses and overhead, you probably have a bad quote on your hands.

Profit

What about profit? Any business owner should be in the business to make money. Profit, which averages single digits for the most successful contractors, is money the contractor should make above and beyond the market value of his physical labor and overhead. Again, if your job quotes do not reflect considerations for the actual cost of the labor, including the contractor's, overhead, and profit, don't be surprised if you struggle getting the job done at all, much less to your standards.

Materials

Let's talk about materials. Is the contractor supplying the materials and if so at what markup – or any markup? Has he factored in the time to secure those materials? At our company we are buying most of our own materials ourselves. We do this through the centralized bid desk of a national home improvement retailer. We do this to control quality, speed up the process, and hopefully save money. We want to get a clearer sense of where our costs are between labor and materials. Is there a right or wrong way? Probably not, but this is what is working for us.

The Lesson Learned

It should be clear at this point that the lowest bid may not be best bid for your project. Having a basic understanding of the business aspects of construction and remodeling is just as important to your profitability as technical understanding or expertise. A great contractor's reference book is *Markup and Profit: A Contractors Guide* by Michael C Stone.

We welcome your thoughts and comments on all aspects of the rehab process. We invite you to post your personal case studies, the good and not-so-good, at www.MyRealEstateLifeOnline.com. The My Real Estate Life™ community offers a wealth of knowledge and experience that will help ensure that all of your projects are profitable.

EXPANDING YOUR PORTFOLIO

PART 6: EXPANDING YOUR PORTFOLIO

The primary reason property management is profitable for us is because many of our clients continue to add to their portfolios over time. They continue to buy, because they are confident in our ability to successfully look after their investments as if they were our own. While property management is a very low margin business, selling additional houses to investors and earning the resulting sales commissions is quite profitable.

We are experts in identifying suitable rental properties for our clients. This is due to our unique experience in the market. Since I first began in 2001, I have actively worked and pursued foreclosed property listings. This work resulted in my team listing well over 1500 distressed properties during the five years after the crash. Many of these properties made several of our property management clients a lot of money. That is something I am very proud of.

These days, in the fall of 2016 as I write this, there is very little distressed inventory on the market for sale. Most of the distressed inventory has finally been depleted. This has caused the average sale price of homes in any given area to go up. However, it has not caused the values of non-distressed homes to rise appreciably outside of hot beds like San Francisco. It is a strange phenomenon. Prices are going up, but individual home owners are not putting their houses on the market to take advantage of the rising market.

We are at historically low inventory levels across the board, and at almost all price points. I believe that while the economy and the jobs situation has improved for many these last few years, it certainly has not improved for all. Consequently, people are either unable to qualify for a mortgage, or if they do qualify, they are unwilling to commit. This is why rental housing is, and will continue to be, such a prudent investment.

The other issue is that, while prices have risen, they have not risen enough to make it possible for many home owners to sell their homes for enough money to pay off their mortgage, cover their selling expenses and secure a down payment on the next home. In other cases, people who do have enough equity to move do not see anything at all on the market they like enough, or can afford to buy.

There is another factor at play right now as well. 2016 is the fourth presidential election year I have experienced since I have been in the real estate business. What I am seeing in the market right now may be more pronounced, but is very much like the slowdown I saw in 2004, 2008, and 2012. Many business and individuals tend to hunker down during election cycles, unwilling to take any perceived risks or make any large investments until the election is over and the new president is in office. It is only natural to want to see how things are going to shake out economically before making a big move – and committing to a thirty year mortgage.

2017 and Beyond

This situation is of course temporary. I expect that 2017 and 2018 could be record setting years in the real estate industry. Notwithstanding a global crises, I believe the stars are aligned for a huge upswing in sales based on an increase in available inventory for sale. People will wake up in 2017 more confident in their futures and will be willing to take reasonable risks to improve their housing situations for themselves and their families. We should also finally start to see millennials settling down and buying homes as we approach 2020.

Another thing I believe we will see in 2017 is the last wave of foreclosed inventory from the financial crises hit the market. We have been sitting with 'zombie' houses in many areas of the country, including Ohio. These are houses that the banks either decided to delay foreclosing on, or did foreclose on but decided for whatever reason not to bring to market. All indications are we will see the last of these abandoned properties list for sale in the next few months. This will be a great buying opportunity for our investors.

I believe there is one other delayed impact of the financial crises that will positively affect inventory levels. The big banks—at the urging of the federal government—modified thousands of mortgages in an effort to keep as many people as possible in their homes after the financial crises. Many of these modifications failed, or are in the process of failing. As the market strengthens, I anticipate the banks will begin to foreclose on these houses.

Investment Funds and Pool Sales

It is a little known fact outside the real estate industry that HUD, Fannie Mae and Freddie Mac disposed of tens of thousands of homes over the last four or five years using what are called 'pool sales'. These government and quasi-government entities were still sitting on inventory three and four years after the crash that would have taken another decade to dispose of one house at a time. This would have potentially delayed the housing recovery. The solution was to group these properties into pools, and sell them to various large investment funds at very attractive prices.

Many of these investment funds immediately got into the property management business and rented them out. They sold off the properties that were uninhabitable as soon as they could while still complying with HUD Guidelines. Now that the market has improved, we will see these funds list and sell these appreciated assets and begin to harvest their profits. We are now seeing listings come in from dozens of investment groups we have never heard of before - in the past, these would have been listings that came to us from Fannie Mae or HUD.

What to Buy and How

By now, you have read throughout this book that the successful investor is going to buy property at prices that will yield a suitable return based on what the population can afford to pay in rent. To do anything else is to bet on appreciation. Betting on appreciation has its place, but not if it means negative cash flow. I am going to discuss in Part 8 of this book how the Space Coast of Florida provides the perfect mix of cash flow and appreciation. In the remainder of this chapter I am going to discuss the actual buying and selling of foreclosed property.

Sourcing New Properties for Purchase

Buying foreclosed properties at a foreclosure auction—or sheriff sale as they are commonly known—is a hit or miss prospect because more often than not the foreclosing bank will bid the price up and buy it themselves. The property will eventually come on the market as an REO property. REO stands for Real Estate Owned and is a term used by banks to refer to housing stock they have in their inventory. The other disadvantage of sheriff sales is that you cannot view the property before bidding. Estate auctions can sometimes yield good buys and you can generally view the property prior to making a bid.

Buying 'short-sales' often worked well in the years immediately following the crash. Most of the major national and regional banks and mortgage companies were willing to allow an owner of record to sell their property for less than was owed because it was a cheaper process than foreclosing. Short sales are less likely to be completed today because the banks have less financial incentive to do so. However, you will still see short sale situations pop up on www.Auction.com prior to the home going to sheriff sale. In my experience, these seldom result in great deals as the goal is to try one last time to make the bank whole.

Properties listed by Realtors® in the Multiple Listing Service (MLS) are by far the best method of sourcing great deals. All of the major government players including the Department of Housing and Urban Development (HUD), Fannie Mae and Freddie Mac list and sell their distressed properties with local real estate firms. Investment firms looking to sell properties they purchased as part of pool sales will list with local real estate firms as well.

The process for purchasing homes is different for each of these entities. HUD, for instance, only allows bids to be placed on the HUD affiliated website HUDHomestore.com. A real estate agent experienced in REO listings and sales will know what is required and can help you get to the closing table regardless of who the seller is.

Owner Occupants and Non-Profits VS Investors

HUD, Fannie Mae, and Freddie Mac all have an initial period of time where they will only accept offers from either certified owner occupants or non-profit organizations. Generally the time frame is a week to 21 days. They will sometimes dictate another owner occupant period after a price reduction.

It is a felony to attempt buy a home as an owner occupant if you are not an owner occupant. If you own property in your name, or in the name of an entity you control you will likely not be considered an owner occupant buyer. The penalties are severe. See below from HUDHomestore.com.

> **What are the penalties for a HUD Home owner-occupant purchaser that does not occupy the property?**
>
> *When a purchaser buys a HUD Home as an owner-occupant, it is expected that the purchaser will live in the property, as his or her primary residence, for a minimum of 12 months. Intentional violation of this requirement could be punishable by a fine not to exceed $250,000 and/or a prison sentence of not more than two years.*
>
> *Source:*
> *www.HUDHomestore.com*

Finding Out About the Best Deals First

A good listing agent will do everything they can to let their past clients know about a new property as soon as it goes on the market. Zillow.com also lists properties that are in foreclosure based on public records but are not yet for sale. The problem with these listings is there is no guarantee they will ever actually be listed for sale. You could be waiting a long time for some of these properties.

The best REO agents have detailed knowledge of what is on the market regardless of who has them listed for sale. These agents tend to have great working relationships with other REO agents and can represent you when you wish to purchase a property.

Your agent also has the ability through their Multiple Listing Service (MLS) to set up an email 'flash' for you. He or she can program your property preferences into the MLS and set it up so that whenever a property is listed which meets your purchase criteria, you will be notified via e-mail immediately.

Working With Your Realtor®

The real estate business is complex and can be very confusing until you understand how real estate agents, Realtors®, and Realtors® who work with REO properties in particular, work together and make a living. The best REO agents are true professionals in every sense of the word. They are bound by, and live by their state's Canon of Ethics and the Realtor® Code of Ethics. We suggest every investor familiarize themselves with the Realtor® Code of Ethics at www.realtor.org.

Every Realtor® is a licensed sales agent or broker in their state. However, not every sales agent is a Realtor®. Licensed sales agents and brokers may list and sell property for other people, and be paid for their services. Unaffiliated sales agents and brokers do not have access to the training and support that Realtors do. More importantly, sales agents who are not Realtors do not have access to the Multiple Listing Service(s) (MLS). This is why working with a Realtor® matters.

First, a couple of facts that may or may not be obvious to you. Real estate agents are independent contractors. Their income is entirely based on the commission they earn. They also pay a portion—if not all—of their own expenses. They only get paid when a property closes.

When a Realtor lists a property, whether for a private individual or an asset management company representing a financial institution, the Realtor's brokerage has a contract to market the property in return for a commission. The commission is split into two parts, the list side and the sell side. Because Realtors cooperate amongst themselves even though they are competitors, hiring a Realtor to list a property extends a financial incentive to every other Realtor in the community to sell the property.

Managing and marketing REO properties is far more intensive than listing and selling properties for private owners. There tends to be a larger personal investment in time and capital because many times the listing agent or brokerage must pay upfront for maintenance and repair costs, and then seek reimbursement from the asset management company. REO listings also require weekly or biweekly inspections and condition reports and Monthly Marketing Reports or MMR's.

There are additional entities involved in the process as well. While a listing agent works directly for a seller, more often than not an REO listing agent works for an asset management company which works for an institutional investor. This adds a layer of complexity, and often frustration to the process. See below:

1. **Bank or Institutional Investor**
   One who owns the property.

2. **Asset Management Company**
   One hired by the bank or institutional investor to manage and sell the property.

3. **Listing Agent**
   The local professional hired by the asset management company.

4. **Selling Agent**
   The local professional representing the buyer. (Sometimes this person is also the listing agent.

5. **The Buyer**

As you can see, the REO listing agent is right in the middle of multiple competing forces with conflicting agendas and goals. Everyone in this process is either looking to make a living, or at the very least, mitigate their losses. The number of participants in the process means that the time it takes an asset manager to respond to offers and counteroffers can vary from not only company to company but property to property. Sadly, listing agents can influence the time-line to some degree, but they have no control over a seller's response time to an offer or counter-offer.

How REO Agents Get Paid

REO commissions are always structured so that all involved are encouraged with financial incentives to find a buyer. REO listing agents generally are required to pay a referral fee back to the asset management company out of the list-side commission for the privilege of marketing the property. However, there is never a referral fee out of the sell-side commission. This results in the sell-side commission often being as much as 50% more than the list-side. The game is structured so that the listing agent will almost always be motivated to sell a property to his or her own clients first.

It is easily the same amount of work, and often less work for the listing agent to sell to their own client as opposed to another agent's client. Having both sides of the deal means the agent can work with someone he knows will close quickly and not waste his time. Perhaps most importantly, when he has both sides of the transaction, he has a better chance of exceeding the expectations of the asset management company that hired him. The better he looks to the asset management company, the more listings he will receive in the future.

Purchase Offers and Negotiations

Knowing how the system works and the motivations and constraints of all the players involved makes you and your agent powerful negotiating partners. When making an offer on an REO property, it is important to be clear on how much the property is worth to you, regardless of what the listing price. As we discussed in Part 4 - Owner Profitability is Job #1, your required return on investment is going to dictate how much you will pay for the property, taking into account any required repairs. If a property is clearly overpriced based on your analysis, it may be best to keep an eye on it and come back in 30 days or so. Most financial institutions start to take price reductions at the 30 day mark. The longer the property sits on the market the more likely the asset manager will be willing to negotiate. On the other hand, some of the smaller players who bought properties in pool sales and are now reselling them may be more receptive to any offer, even a low-ball offer.

I consider a low ball offer to be 80% or less of the list price. Keep in mind, you run the risk of damaging your reputation as a qualified buyer if you continuously make low ball offers on properties listed with the same agent or owned by the same financial institution. Your agent, the listing agent and the asset manager answering directly to the bank that owns the property, are all very busy people. The last thing you want to do is damage what could be a very profitable relationship for you by wasting their time.

Listen to the advice and counsel of your agent. If the listing agent even hints that the seller is looking for offers, consider it an invitation to make whatever offer makes sense for you. Even if the seller cannot sell at your price today they may be able work with you later. In this situation, you are actually helping both the listing agent and the asset manager.

Multiple Offer Situations

Just as some properties are initially priced too high when they come on the market and take a long time to sell, some properties are listed too low. These too good to be true listings are the ones everyone dreams about. These listings almost always have a lot of action and result in multiple offers.

Multiple offer situations can be tricky to navigate. Most asset managers will ask all parties to make their highest and best offer after a certain number of days on the market. Other asset managers will decide to only negotiate with the very best offer or the best two or three offers and simply reject, or ignore for as long as they can, the other offers. Multiple offer situations can be aggravating for buyers who do not understand the legalities of these situations.

The following are excerpts from two articles from the Ohio Association of Realtors regarding multiple offers.

Legally speaking: Is notification required when multiple offers are received?

Q: If I receive multiple offers on my listing, am I required to notify all of the agents/buyers that they are in a multiple offer situation?

A: Even though there is nothing in the license law that requires such disclosure, many agents believe doing so is a good idea for two reasons. First, they believe this is fair to all of the parties involved. Secondly, they believe that making all parties aware of this situation is in the seller's best interests because it could cause the buyers to increase their offers.

While both of these may be true, disclosing that there are multiple offers could result in one or more of the buyers withdrawing their offer because they don't want to be in a "bidding war." If this occurs, it is certainly not in the seller's best interests. More importantly, the fact that the seller has received other offers could be considered confidential information. For these reasons the fact that there are multiple offers should not be disclosed without explaining to the seller the benefits and risks of such disclosure and obtaining the seller's informed consent.

Standard of Practice 1-15 of NAR's Code of Ethics likewise provides that the existence of other offers can only be disclosed if the listing agent has the seller's consent to do so. However S.O.P. 1-15 goes a little further. It provides that if the seller authorizes the listing agent to disclose that there are multiple offers, that the listing agent must also disclose whether the other offers were written by the listing agent, another agent in the same brokerage or a cooperating agent — but this is only required if the listing agent is asked who wrote the other offers.

August 5, 2013 by Peg Ritenour, OAR Vice President of Legal Services/Administration

http://ohiorealtors.org/2013/08/05/legally-speaking-is-notification-required-when-multiple-offers-are-received/

More on Multiple Offers from the Ohio Association of Realtors

1. A listing agent describes an offer to an out-of-town seller over the telephone. The seller verbally indicates his acceptance of that offer, which the listing agent communicates to the buyer. Before the seller receives and signs the original offer, the listing agent receives another offer, which the seller wants to accept. Is there a binding contract with the first buyer?

Answer: No. Although the seller verbally accepted the first offer, under the Statute of Frauds there would not be a binding contract because the seller did not sign the offer. Therefore, the seller would be free to accept the second offer.

2. Negotiations have been going back and forth between a seller and a buyer for over a week. The seller is considering a counteroffer from this buyer, when another higher offer is received. Is the listing agent required to notify the first buyer that another offer has been received and give that buyer an opportunity to increase his counteroffer?

Answer: No, there is nothing that legally requires the seller to give the first buyer an opportunity to raise his offer. Of course, if the seller wishes to give the first buyer such an opportunity, he may do so, and the listing agent would have to follow these instructions.

3. A listing agent has received an offer which he is planning on presenting to the seller that afternoon. Before she makes this presentation she is notified by a cooperating agent that another buyer will probably be making an offer the next day. Should the listing agent wait until this second offer is received to present the first offer?

Answer: The listing agent must present the first offer she has received as soon as possible. Therefore, she should present the first offer that afternoon as planned. However, her fiduciary duties to the seller also require her to notify the seller that another offer may be forthcoming. It will then be up to the seller to decide whether he wants to wait for this offer. This listing agent should review the first offer to determine how long it is open for acceptance, so that it does not expire before the seller decides to accept or counter it.

4. A seller has received two offers to purchase his property. Can he make counteroffers to both buyers?

Answer: While he can do this, it is not recommended for the seller to make more than one counteroffer at a time. This is because both buyers could accept the counteroffer and deliver notice.

5. An offer is presented to the seller which is signed by the seller. The listing agent immediately calls the buyer and leaves a message on the buyer's answering machine that the seller has accepted his offer. The buyer receives this message. Five minutes after the seller signed the offer, another offer is received which is higher than the signed offer. Can the seller accept the higher offer or is he bound to the contract he signed? The contract is silent regarding the method and delivery of acceptance.

Answer: The seller accepted the offer by signing the contract. To have a binding contract the seller's acceptance must be communicated to the buyer. As the contract does not require that the communication be by physically returning the signed contract to the buyer, verbal notification to the buyer, would be sufficient. Therefore, the sellers have entered into a binding contract with the first buyer.

6. If I receive multiple offers on one of my listings, must I notify all of the agents/buyers that they are in a multiple offer situation?

Answer: There is nothing in the license law that requires such disclosure. Most agents do so because they believe it is the fair way to handle negotiations and that it could get the buyers to increase their offers. While this may be true, disclosing that there are multiple offers could result in one or more of the buyers withdrawing their offer because they don't want to be in a "bidding war." For this reason, Standard of Practice 1-15 of NAR's Code of Ethics states the existence of other offers should only be disclosed with the seller's consent.

http://ohiorealtors.org/legal/topics/contracts/multiple-offers

Earnest Money and Proof of Funds

Most REO listings result in cash only contracts. Asset managers prefer a cash sale because the process is quicker and cleaner. The purchase contract will stipulate that the sale is for a property in as-is condition, meaning the seller will make no repairs. Asset managers will accept cash offer over financed offers because the appraisal and loan process is fraught with unknowns that could delay or kill the deal. The resulting additional time on market can adversely affect an asset manager's performance and compensation.

Proof of funds are required with all initial purchase offers and the funds must be in the name of the person or entity who is making the offer. As a rule, earnest money equivalent to 10% of the purchase price or $1,000 whichever is greater will be required by the seller. Once the contract is ratified, the earnest money will be exchanged in the form of a certified check as outlined in the contract.

Conclusion

An experienced real estate professional can work with you to expand your portfolio by helping to identify and evaluate potentially great new investments for you. More importantly, they can help you navigate the complexities of an REO purchase and get you to the closing table. My hope is that this information will help you profitably expand your portfolio.

LOW BALL VS. REASONABLE OFFERS - APRIL 2009

Many buyers right now think that they have to write low ball offers on foreclosed properties to get a great deal. This can be self-defeating as the majority of foreclosed listings are priced to move already. When preparing an offer keep in mind the following basics

- What is your MAO or Maximum Allowable Offer? The list price of the property should have no bearing at all on you calculations.

- If you can buy the house at your MAO then it is by definition a good deal. Can you make it a better deal by buying for less? Of course, but that is just icing on the cake

- What constitutes a 'low ball' offer? In our experience as listing and selling agents of REO properties, anything less than 80% of list is a low ball offer.

In the past we found that the longer a property is on the market, the more likely it is a 'weak' or 'low ball' offer will be considered. However, this truism is changing as banks and investors become more motivated to minimize their losses with a quick sale. Countywide Mortgage's current pricing policy is a good example.

Brad, I, and The Mid Ohio REO Team, list and sell foreclosed properties for Countrywide through various asset management companies in the Springfield/Dayton, Ohio areas. Countrywide and other loan servicers and investors are far more attuned to the local market than in the past. They are paying more attention to what the local Realtors and appraisers opinions of value are which is reflected in the initial list prices.

Not only are we seeing better initial list prices, we are seeing price reductions come through as frequently as every two to three weeks versus up to 90 days in the past. Consequently, the banks are less likely to entertain low ball offers because they are receiving multiple reasonable offers with every price reduction. Most accepted offers are within 5% of full price if cash, and even closer to full price if financed. (Cash is indeed king right now due to the number of financed deals that are falling through.)

The message here is, know your market, know your trends and comparables, and stick to your numbers. If your numbers indicate a full price or better offer, make your highest and best offer up front. You will increase your chances of successfully negotiating a purchase.

What are you seeing? What are you hearing from you agents/Realtor partners? Share your experiences with the www.MyRealEstateLifeOnline.com community.

SHERIFF'S SALE OPPORTUNITIES — OR A WASTE OF INVESTORS' TIME? JUNE 8, 2009

As we have talked about many times in the past, we have never had much luck buying property at Sheriff's sale because the investor/bank generally comes in and bids the property up past the point where a purchase for us makes sense. I still don't understand the rationale for this process but I believe it has to do with when the investor/bank chooses to show a loss on their books.

The cost of running many of these properties through the REO process is very high and it often seems that the bank would be better off taking their hit up front. However, I am not complaining, we have made a lot of money on REO properties over the years.

In some instances however, rationality may be slowly creeping into the process, to the chagrin of property owners, municipalities, and ultimately investors. A March 30, 2009 article in the New York Times entitled "Banks Starting to Walk Away on Foreclosures" describes a situation in South Bend, Indiana, where the bank walked away from a property already scheduled for sheriff sale.

This action has left the city to clean up the mess and the homeowner to foot the bill. In this case, the owner had already suffered the pre-foreclosure process and thought the episode was behind her when the sheriff's sale was cancelled at the last minute. She still owns the house but owes the city money for maintaining it and ultimately demolishing it.

According to the article, this is happening all over the country. How is this potentially good for the savvy investor? Strictly speaking it is not because if the sheriff's sale is canceled, nobody is going to buy the property. So the question remains, why do we continue to go to sheriff's sale almost every Friday morning?

In Springfield, Ohio, where we live and work, one of my partners recently picked up a house at sheriff's sale and it was a surprisingly good deal. A fluke? Maybe. However, Brad reported last week that a handful of properties went to sale and the banks did not show up to bid the property up as they normally do. This of course made it possible for an investor to make a purchase at a reasonable price. Why didn't the banks show up? We have no idea.

So much about this foreclosure crisis is changing daily. It is almost impossible to keep up. But just when we thought it was time to formally take sheriff sale due diligence off of our weekly to-do lists, we see reason to continue following the process.

WHERE HAVE ALL THE FORECLOSURES GONE? MARCH 2009

The number of sheriff sales in Springfield, Ohio has dropped in recent months, even as our local economy has fallen off a cliff since September. I have heard that his is happening elsewhere and may be the result of the Fannie and Freddie, holiday eviction moratorium, HOPE Now programs, and other local, national, public and private initiatives.

Our REO listing inventory in Dayton and Springfield spiked in December 2008, and January 2009. It has currently leveled off concurrent with fewer sheriff sales.

Does this mean the foreclosure crises is over? I doubt it, but I am not sure why we are in this lull either – especially when vacant housing stock is at an all-time high. Dayton, Ohio was recently highlighted as the fourth most vacant city in America.

One theory is that the banks are so overwhelmed that they are paralyzed. Another is that given how the loans were sold, identifying the actual owners of the properties is time consuming and problematic. A third and perhaps more cynical explanation is that the banks are holding back on foreclosures and sales in an effort to protect their bottom lines.

The argument goes that an entity only has to show a loss when it experiences a loss. Regardless of the value of the asset on the balance sheet, there is no operating loss until it is sold. With this in mind it makes sense that there was a burst of activity near the end of the banks' fiscal year. It also makes sense that until lending stabilizes to the point that there are clear and consistent operating profits, that banks would keep these assets on the books until they are able to 'hide' the losses amidst new profits

In any case, I believe there will be more foreclosed housing stock hitting the market in the next few months. On the other hand, this anecdotal experience may mean that investors who wish to buy low and hold, need to get off the fence and into the game sooner rather than later.

THE BASICS OF MANAGEMENT

PART 7: THE BASICS OF MANAGEMENT— HOW WE DO IT

As I have discussed throughout this book this is the best of times for residential property owners, provided they have the business partnerships and/or infrastructure in place to ensure the assets perform as desired. The historically 'Mom and Pop' structure of the management business must give way to efficient and effective systems and processes. The opportunity for professionalizing the property management business has presented itself, and that is why I am in this business.

This also means, however, that all property managers, including our team at ROOST, have to continue to raise the bar on our performance and the services we provide. We take our job as the intermediary—the licensed real estate broker between the tenant client and the investor client—very seriously. This chapter discusses how we go about that business.

Why We Do It

Property management has never been easy. For the most part, it has been a niche business for a handful of small real estate firms. However, demand for this service is rising. The challenge is serving the needs of the tenant-client while ensuring that the owner-client is making the required return on his or her investment.

Prudent application of technology and the realization that many tenant clients will become buyers—and if not buyers then potentially tenants for life—means that incorporating property management into the traditional brokerage model is an opportunity whose time has come. As we have previously discussed, our owner clients are some of the best clients and referral sources we have. These relationships are also the source of a lot of sales business as they continue to add to their portfolio over time.

How We Split Tasks

One true secret of our success in this business are the detailed job descriptions that we have developed over the years. The job descriptions are updated from time to time as circumstances change, but they always reflect what we know works. Detailed job descriptions provide myriad benefits. They keep us on task and communicate and remind new and existing team members what is expected of them.

When we have a job opening, we hire to the job description. We use the job description to describe the position when we advertise for help, and we use it as the basis for assessing performance. Every team member has every other team member's job description, so they know how they all must work together to take care of our owners and tenants.

As you will see in the job descriptions that follow, we have learned over the years that the most effective way of getting the job done is to split the department into three distinct categories. The team members in each category all have distinct and unique abilities that form a 'Unique Ability Team'. These categories are:

- Landlord Support
- Tenant Relations
- Accounting

The more we can keep key team members focused solely on their areas of responsibility, the more smoothly the team runs. However, we do believe in cross training everybody, because quite frankly, things change and people leave us. Sometimes our volume ramps up before we have a chance to hire to support it and everyone has to pitch in to help. A temporary 'blurring' of the job descriptions is sometimes appropriate and unavoidable. As always, the sooner we get everyone back to their unique abilities and doing what they were hired to do, the happier we all are.

Another tool we use that helps us hire to the job descriptions is the Kolbe B Index (www.Kolbe.com). The Kolbe B provides a profile for each of our employees that measures what is called conative ability. It does not measure IQ or motivation, but details how a person goes about their work.

At this point, we have good history regarding our current and past team members' Kolbe profiles. We know what success looks like. This allows us to interview people using the job description as a guide, and based on the initial interview, select applicants to take the Kolbe B assessment on line. Based on the applicants Kolbe results, we know if they are a right fit for the job at hand.

In addition to the Kolbe, we also have created our own in-house tests. We have one for breaking down an tenant application, running credit and criminal background checks, and calling references. We have another that asks the applicant to break down last week's maintenance payroll and assign it to the various owners for reimbursement. The results of this process give us a pretty good idea as to whether someone is going to be successful or not in their role.

Job Descriptions

Property Manager/Landlord Support

- Bring consistency, quality control, and creativity to our client experience.
- Maintain minimum 95% Rent Collected Standard each month
- Add new owner clients.
- Work with owners and tenants to maximize the rent collected each month.
- Meet the Maintenance Staff weekly and additionally as needed to coordinate completion of the maintenance log.
- Mowing and Utility lists.

- Perform Inspections, create punch lists, and solicit bids.

- Update AppFolio Notes with all activity. Move outs', move in's, owner adds and property adds.

- Recommend prospective tenants to landlords based on application, credit and criminal background, and income/ability to pay.

- Lease renewals performed monthly.

Landlord Support Administrative Assistant

- Works directly for the Property Manager

- Property Manager/Tenant Relations Specialist

- Maintain minimum 95% Rent Collected Standard each month

- Review maintenance requests daily and coordinate repairs with the maintenance staff.

- Negotiate leases and get signatures.

- Write and post three day notices, complete eviction paperwork and attend court.

- Recommend prospective tenants based on application, credit and criminal background, and income/ability to pay.

- Show properties as needed.

- Pest control inspections and estimates.

- Section 8 inspections and estimates.

- Advertising on AppFolio and Vacant Property Sheet

- Copy keys.
- Attend eviction court.
- Complete inspections for occupied properties.
- PM filing and keys and documents.

Tenant Relations Administrative Assistant

- Maintain a professional atmosphere in the reception and office areas at all times. Keep office tidy and keep trash removed.
- Answer the phone by third ring each time. Good Afternoon ROOST Real Estate Co. how may I help you?
- Greet walk in traffic
- Accept rent and turn in to accounting. VERIFY INITIAL NEXT TO TENANT NAME AND ADDRESS ON EACH CHECK OR MONEY ORDER BEFORE TURNING IN TO ACCOUNTING.
- Collect rental applications and application fee(s).
- Make copies, send faxes, scan, and email, cover other team members as needed.
- Respond to rental calls and emails. (See Non-Licensed White Paper)
- Filing - keys and paperwork
- Keep AppFolio marketing website updated.
- Assist property manager with bids and to-dos as needed.

Accounting Manager

- Compliance. Audit/Balance Property Management, Operating and Trust Accounts.

- Client Relations. Be available to discuss profit and loss statements with landlord clients.

Accounting/Bookkeeping Assistant

- Retrieve, open and distribute mail.

- Processes rent, accounts receivable, and accounts payable.

- Add rent to Google Sheet.

- Create monthly reports for owners.

- Make copies, send faxes, scan, and email, cover other team members as needed.

- Process time cards for payroll reimbursement by owners.

- Match REO reimbursement checks with invoices.

- Cover front desk from 5 to 6 and alternate Saturdays.

- Check night drop and make post office runs.

- Filing keys and documents.

- Cover front desk as needed.

- Run rental applications when needed.

- Make AppFolio changes for Section 8 awards and changes in rent.

- Work the 'Singles'.

- Lease renewals and increases.
    - Calculate new rent.
    - Update AppFolio.
    - Create new lease and cover letter.
    - 60 days out.
    - Calls to approve or deny applications

Accounting/Bookkeeping Assistant

Bring consistency, quality control, and creativity to our client experience.

- Retrieve, open and distribute mail.
- Processes rent, accounts receivable, and accounts payable.
- Work the accounts payable 'Trays'.
- Create monthly reports for owners.
- Make copies, send faxes, scan, and email, cover other teammembers as needed.
- Process time cards for payroll reimbursement by owners.
- Match reimbursement checks with invoices.
- Cover front desk as needed.
- Check night drop and make bank and post office runs.
- Filing keys and documents.
- Run rental applications when needed.

- Charge back landlord clients payroll and materials.
- Prepare monthly reports for landlords.
- Reimburse payroll
- Make deposits.

AppFolio Specialist

- Train Bookkeeping Assistants and Property Managers as needed.
- Assist Accounting Manager identifying and correcting errors.
- Audit move in/move out's.
- Insure new owners and properties are set up properly.
- Make changes to AppFolio set-up as needed/when system is upgraded.
- Set up new market portfolios as required. (Florida)
- Ensure monthly reconciliation reports are prepared for sign off by the broker for both Florida and Ohio.

Internal and External Team Members

These job descriptions reflect our employees, or what I think of as our Internal team members. Our actual team is much larger when you consider all of the External team members that work with us as independent contractors and service providers. These indispensable members of our team include:

- Dedicated Appfolio Accountant
- Our Accountants and Tax Advisors

- 1099 Construction Contractors
- Plumbers, HVAC, Roofers and assorted maintenance Life Savers
- Container and Trash Hauling Service
- Ray at the Water Department
- Our Banking Partners
- Appfolio Help Desk and Sales
- Rently Representative
- Real Estate Attorney on Retainer
- Eviction Attorney
- And many more.....

Marketing Our Rental Properties

In Springfield, we are fortunate to have a steady stream of incoming referrals and repeat clients that rent our properties. 99% of our advertising and marketing efforts are online. We also place yard signs on each property, generating hundreds of additional calls a week

Our For Rent Signs

OUR WEBSITES

We do extensive internet marketing using our websites www.ROOSTRentals4u.com in Ohio and www.ROOSTRentals.com in Florida. Our sites are populated with a feed from our software partners Appfolio. By using Appfolio, our listings automatically go to hundreds of rental websites including Zillow. Our listing exposure is second to none. Here is a description of the service from the Appfolio website:

Posting Vacancy Ads

When all of your property information is stored in AppFolio, marketing vacant units is quick and easy because you save so much time and avoid the hassle of maintaining information in multiple locations. In just a few clicks you can quickly post your vacancies to hundreds of sites on the Internet including your own website, Oodle, Rentals.com, Apartments.com, Zillow and Trulia, to name just a few. You can also download professionally formatted HTML code and images to use when manually posting to listing sites like Craigslist.

Posting to Rental Listing Sites is Easy

Manually posting to rental listing sites outside of AppFolio can take hours each week—we've even talked with customers who used to spend a day or more on postings. AppFolio saves you valuable time by being able to post to hundreds of listing sites with a click of a button. With this ability and the option for prospects to fill out a Guest Card or to Apply Online, you can now speed up the leasing flow and fill your vacancies faster.

Monitor Your Marketing from One Place

We also provide reports that help you track the success of your marketing efforts. You can track guest cards by lead source, you can easily see and pay closer attention to those units that have been vacant the longest and see what happens over time as you change the language of your ads, change market rent or highlight different amenities.

*Source:
www.appfolio.com*

The Application and Screening Process

We encourage people to apply online whenever we can. Our online application and screening services are also provided by our software partners Appfolio. Our applicants can also fill out our application form and mail it in or drop it off at the office. The act of successfully and completely filling out the application is a screening step in and of itself. The non-refundable application fee is also an important piece of the process that discourages applicants from applying who do not meet our criteria.

Our applications include the disclosure that we will perform credit and criminal background checks on every adult applicant. The applicants' signatures give us consent to run these reports. Fairness and consistency in this process is paramount because it is first good business, and second, it ensures we do not run afoul of any Fair Housing laws.

How We Show Properties

In almost all cases viewing our available rental listings is a self-serve process. On in-town listings, the applicant can come into our office and leave their driver's license with us and get a key to the property. We have used this method for years and never had a problem.

On other listings, we use an electronic lockbox service called Rently (www.Rently.com). The Rently app can be downloaded to a smart phone. The applicant supplies Rently with a credit card number and in return they get an access code to the lockbox. It is secure and convenient, and we are expanding this service with additional boxes every month. Here is a description of the service from the Rently website:

What is Rently?

Rently is a premier lockbox rental showing solution. Utilizing Rently's lockbox rental solution renters can instantly and securely access properties at their convenience. This method, also referred to as Self Service Showing, is becoming the industry norm as property managers save money and lease faster than ever before.

Get More Leads

Using Rently, you're going to generate more leads than ever before. With our system, every day is an open house and renters will be able to see your properties at the time that best fits their needs. Self-service showings equal more qualified leads coming in around the clock: even during afterhours and weekends. More leads in less time means you'll be leasing faster!

Manage More Properties

Because you and your agents won't have to be physically present during the showing process, you'll be able to spend more time focusing on signing new business and growing your company. Allowing Renters to view your vacant unit at their convenience gives you a competitive advantage and will have you leasing faster. More owners will want to use your management services. Leasing has never been easier.

Lease Faster

With the Rently system, you will get more leads in a shorter amount of time. Renters are eager to find a new home and by eliminating delay between renter interest and property showing, you'll be leasing faster. The Rently system will significantly reduce your property's time on market.

Source:
www.use.rently.com

Security Deposits

Generally we suggest our owners ask for a security deposit equal to the monthly rent amount when they lease their properties with us. Once we approve an applicant, we ask them for the security deposit prior to signing the lease and collecting the first month's rent. The security deposit is non-refundable. We do not want to take a property off the market without some assurance that they will indeed sign the lease on the agreed upon date.

If the tenant fulfills the terms of the lease and leaves the property damage free and broom swept, they will be refunded their deposit within 30 days. In Ohio, the security deposits can go to the owner or they can stay in our property management trust account. In Florida, tenant deposits must be kept in a separate property management escrow account.

APPLICATION

1. PLEASE INCLUDE A $40 APPLICATION FEE FOR ONE APPLICANT IN THE EXACT AMOUNT. PLEASE INCLUDE A $60 APPLICATION FEE FOR TWO APPLICANTS IN THE EXACT AMOUNT. PLEASE INCLUDE A $100 APPLICATION FEE FOR THREE APPLICANTS. PLEASE INCLUDE A $120 APPLICATION FEE FOR FOUR APPLICANTS. **MONEY ORDER ONLY**. THIS IS **NON-REFUNDABLE** WHETHER THE APPLICANT IS DENIED OR APPROVED.

2. PLEASE INCLUDE ALL PROOF OF INCOME FOR THE LAST 3 MONTHS. (CHECK STUBS, SSI, FEDERAL AID, ETC.) EXAMPLE: IF THE CURRENT MONTH IS MAY, INCLUDE ALL CHECK STUBS FOR ALL OF FEBRUARY, MARCH, AND APRIL WHAT YOU HAVE RECEIVED SO FAR IN MAY. EACH APPLICANT NEEDS TO SUPPLY THEIR OWN INCOME.

3. INCOME REQUIREMENT: YOUR MONTHLY NET INCOME MUST BE 3 TIMES THE RENT AMOUNT TO QUALIFY. EX: IF RENT IS OVER $500 A MONTH, YOUR MONTHLY INCOME MUST BE AT LEAST $1500 A MONTH TO QUALIFY.

4. EACH ADULT THAT WILL BE LIVING IN THE HOME NEEDS TO COMPLETE AN APPLICATION. IF ONE ADULT IS APPLYING, A $40 APPLICATION FEE NEEDS TO BE SUBMITTED. IF TWO ADULTS ARE APPLYING, A $60 APPLICATION FEE NEEDS TO BE SUBMITTED. IF THREE ADULTS ARE APPLYING, A $100 APPLICATION FEE NEEDS TO BE SUBMITTED. IF FOUR ADULTS ARE APPLYING, A $120 APPLICATION FEE NEEDS TO BE SUBMITTED.

5. **<u>APPLICATION FEES ARE NOT REFUNDABLE AT ANY TIME.</u>**

6. ALL APPLICATIONS MUST BE COMPLETED IN FULL. THIS INCLUDES CURRENT AND PREVIOUS LANDLORD INFORMATION

AND PHONE NUMBERS. ANY FALSE INFORMATION GIVEN WILL RESULT IN THE APPLICATION BEING DENIED.

ROOST REAL ESTATE Co. Rental Application

14 E. Main St. Springfield, OH 45502
Voice 937-390-3715 Fax 937-390-0112

EACH APPLICANT MUST COMPLETE A SEPARATE APPLICATION
All information must be completed.

Address you are applying for: _____

Date you want to move in: _____

How did you hear about us? _____

Why do you want to leave where you live now? _____

Have you ever been on a lease? _____

Are you being evicted now? _____

Have you ever been evicted? _____

If so why? _____

How much rent can you pay each month? _____

Who else will be living in the property with you? _____

Have you ever been convicted of a crime? _____

If so please explain_____

Do you have a pet? If so what type and how much does it weigh?

_____

YOUR PERSONAL INFORMATION

Full Name (Include Middle Initial) _____

Date of Birth _____ Email Address _____

Phone (____) _____ Work Phone (____) _____

Cell Phone (____) _____

Social Security Number _____-_____-_____

Driver's License # _____ State _____

Present Address _____

City _____ State _____ Zip _____

2

A Real Estate Investor's Guide to Profitability

How Long? _____ if renting, apartment name/location: _____ _____

Are you on a lease? _____ Are you month-to-month? _____ Is this Family? _____

_____

Current Payment $_____

Landlord/mgr.'s name_____Phone (____) _____

Previous Address _____

City _____State _____ Zip _____

How Long? _____ If renting, Apartment name/location _____

Are you on a lease? _____ Are you month-to-month? _____ Is this Family? _____

_____

Previous Payment $_____

Landlord/mgr.'s name_____Phone (____) _____

Employer _____

Position _____How long? _____

Address_____

Phone (____) _____

Previous Employer_____

Position _____How long? _____

Address_____

Phone (____) _____

Gross Monthly Income before Deductions _____

Bank_____

Personal Reference(s) _____ Phone #_____

Professional Reference (s) _____ Phone #_____

I declare that the application is complete, true and correct and I herewith give my permission for anyone contacted to release the credit or personal information of the undersigned applicant to Management or their authorized agents, at any time, for the purposes of entering into and continuing to offer or collect on any agreement and/or credit extended. I further authorize Management or their Authorized Agents to verify the application information including but not limited to obtaining criminal records, contacting creditors, present or former landlords, employers and personal references, whether listed or not, at the time of the application and at any time in the future, with regard to any agreement entered into with Management. Any false information will constitute grounds for rejection of this application, or Management may at any time immediately terminate any agreement entered into in reliance upon misinformation given on this application.

I understand that the $40.00 application fee is non-refundable whether the application is denied or approved. If the application is approved and you have paid the deposit but neglect to sign the lease the deposit will be forfeited.

_____
Applicant(s) Signature and Date

**************EACH APPLICANT MUST COMPLETE A SEPARATE APPLICATION************************

The Leasing Package

We prefer to meet our tenants face to face when we sign a lease. We can sign leases electronically, but for most tenants we believe it is helpful to sit down with them and go over what we expect from them and what they can expect from us. The lease package consists of:

- The ROOST Way Brochure™
- Lead Based Paint Addendum and Brochure (If Applicable)
- Crime Free Lease Addendum
- Smoke Alarm Agreement
- Local Tenants Rights Brochure and sign off sheet.
- Notification Regarding Renter's Insurance
- Water Card
- The Lease
- Deposit Form
- A Checklist for the meeting.

STANDARD REAL ESTATE RENTAL AGREEMENT

This Lease/Agreement made this day:_____
Owner / Manager: **ROOST Real Estate Co.**
Tenant **/** Resident:_____
Property located at_____

_____ **1. TERM:** Agreement shall be for **one year** beginning on the **1st day of September 2016** and ending the **31st of August 2017.**

_____**2. POSSESSION:** Should Management be unable to deliver possession of the Property at the commencement of this Agreement, Management shall not be liable for damages caused thereby, nor shall this agreement be void, but Resident shall not be liable for any rent until possession is delivered. Resident may terminate this Agreement if possession is not delivered within seven (7) days of the start of the term hereof.

_____**3. RENT:** Rent **($375.00) per month** due on the **1st** day of each and every month during the initial or any extended term of this Agreement, and shall be annually adjusted. Unless otherwise notified in writing, the monthly rental payment shall increase annually by ten percent (10%) payable monthly beginning the month following the initial term and adjusting annually thereafter. Rental payments shall be made at the office of Management or such other place as Management may from time to time designate. **MAILING THE RENT BY THE DUE DATE DOES NOT CONSTITUTE PAYMENT. RENTS MUST BE <u>RECEIVED</u> at the office of the Management BEFORE <u>DUE DATE</u> of each month to be considered paid. Monies received are applied first to any outstanding additional rent; second to any unpaid fees or charges, then third to any current rent or rent to become due. This could result in unpaid rent which would be subject to additional rent as contained herein. Cash will not be accepted. Money orders or checks shall be made payable to: ROOST Real Estate Co. P.O. Box 2699 Springfield, OH 45501 RENT DUE ON 1ST, LATE ON 6TH, EVICTION ON 10TH UNLESS PAYMENT ARRANGEMENTS HAVE BEEN MADE WITH PROPERTY MANAGER. PARTIAL PAYMENTS WILL NOT BE ACCEPTED.**

_____ **4. ADDITIONAL RENT & RETURNED CHECKS:** If Management elects to accept rent after the **5TH** day of the month, resident agrees to pay **10% of rent late fee.** In the event any check is returned by the bank unpaid, Resident agrees to pay to Management bank NSF fees. Any returned check must be redeemed by cashier's check, certified check or money order. In the event more than one check is returned, Resident herewith agrees to pay all future rents and charges in the form of cashier's check, certified check or money order.

_____ **5. DEPOSIT:** The resident has paid a deposit of **($375.00)** Said deposit shall be returned at the end of the rental period when unit is found to be in good condition, 30 day written notice is given, and all agreements have been met.

____ **6. CONDITION:** Resident accepts Property in its present **"AS-IS"** condition, and has been given the right to inspect the property, and has approved said property. Resident acknowledges that the premises are in good order and repair, unless otherwise indicated in writing. Resident shall, at his own expense, and at all times, maintain the premises in a clean and sanitary manner, including all equipment and appliances therein and shall surrender the same, at the termination hereof, in as good condition as received, normal wear and tear excepted. Resident also agrees to change the furnace filter every 3 months. Resident shall further keep and maintain all interior and exterior portions of the Premises, the sidewalks and drives on or about the Premises in a clean, and sanitary condition, and free of ice and snow. Lessee shall keep the lawn mowed, shrubbery trimmed and the yard free of excessive weed growth, so that the lawn and yard shall at all times be maintained in a neat and presentable condition.

____ **7. UTILITIES:** Resident shall obtain and pay for all utility services including gas, heat, electricity, water, sewer and trash removal and any other utility used or consumed on the premises by resident. **Billing responsibility for all utilities to be placed in Residents name at the commencement of the Agreement.**

____ **8. APPLIANCES:** All appliances of any kind including window air conditioners are specifically excluded from this Agreement. Such appliances remain as a convenience to Resident and Management assumes no responsibility for their operation. No part of the monthly rent is attributable to them. Any appliance on premises at the signing of this Agreement shall be returned by Resident upon move-out in the same condition as at the signing of this Agreement (**unless appliances are furnished by tenant)**.

____ **9. ALTERATIONS:** Resident shall not make, or allow to be made, any alterations, installations, or redecoration of any kind to the Property without prior written permission of Management, provided, however, that notwithstanding such consent, Resident agrees that all alterations including, without limitation, any items affixed to the Property, shall become the property of Management upon the termination of this Agreement. This includes, but is not limited to, ceiling fans, mini blinds, carpeting, fencing, lighting fixtures, shrubs, flowers, etc. Removal of these items shall be considered theft subject to civil and criminal prosecution.

____ **10. USE:** The Property shall be used for Residential purposes only shall be occupied by the undersigned adults and children as named in the original application to rent, **only**. Resident shall not use the Property or permit it to be used for any disorderly or unlawful purpose or in any manner so as to interfere with the quiet peaceful enjoyment of the neighborhood. Resident shall be responsible and fully liable for the conduct of his/her guests. Acts of guests in violation of this Agreement or Management's rules and regulations may be deemed by Management to be a breach by Resident.

____**11. SMOKE DETECTORS:** Resident acknowledges the presence of a working smoke detector in the premises, and agrees to test the detector weekly for proper operation, and further agrees to replace any batteries (if so equipped) when necessary. Resident further acknowledges that he/she understands how to test and operate the smoke detector in this Property. Resident also agrees to notify the manager of any inoperative smoke detector immediately so if can be replaced.

____ **12. EVICTION:** If rent has not been paid when due, then Management shall automatically and immediately have the right to assert all legal and contractual remedies to enforce this agreement.

_____ **13. FAILURE OF MANAGEMENT TO ACT:** Failure of Management to insist upon strict compliance with the terms of this Agreement shall not constitute a waiver of any violation, nor shall any acceptance of a partial payment of rent be deemed a waiver of Management's right to full amount.

____ **14. ACCURACY AND RESPONSIBILITY:** Management has relied upon the information contained in Resident's application to enter into this Agreement. Resident warrants that their rental application is true, complete and accurate. Resident agrees that if he/she has falsified any statement in the rental application, Management has the right to terminate this Rental Agreement immediately and further agrees that Management shall be entitled to retain any deposit. In the event of default by any one Resident, each and every remaining Resident shall be responsible for timely payment of full rent and all other provisions of this Agreement.

_____ **15. INDEMNIFICATION:** Management shall not be liable for any damage or injury to Resident, or any other person, or to any property, occurring on the Property, or any part thereof, or in common areas thereof, unless such damage is the proximate result of the negligence or unlawful act of Management, his agents, or his employees. Resident does hereby indemnify, release, and save harmless Management and Management agents from and against any and all suits, actions, claims, judgments, and expenses arising out of or relating to any loss of life, bodily or personal injury, property damage, or other demand, claim or action of any nature arising out of or related to this Agreement or the use of this Property and premises.

____ **16. SEVERABILITY:** In the event that any part of this Agreement be construed as unenforceable, the remaining parts of this Agreement shall remain in full force and effect as though the unenforceable part or parts were not written into this Agreement.

____ **17. GENDER:** All references to Resident herein employed shall be construed to include the plural as well as the singular, and the masculine shall include the feminine and neuter where the context of this Agreement may require.

____ **18. ENTIRE AGREEMENT:** This Agreement and any attached addendum constitutes the sole and entire Agreement between the parties and no representation, promise, or inducement not included in this Agreement, oral or written, shall be binding upon any party hereto. Attachments: EPA Lead Paint Disclosure; EPA Lead Paint Pamphlet; Other:

____ **19. PEST CONTROL**: You are responsible to keep the premises free of pest and pay for pest control services if such services are needed. Management has the right to accept money from the tenant and apply it to a previous pest control invoice.

____ **20. PETS:**

____ 21. **AUTOMOBILES:** Non-working automobiles are not allowed to be parked at the residence. All non-working vehicles will be towed at the owner's expense.

____ 22. **SATILLITES:** Resident is not permitted to give permission to cable/internet companies to install a satellite dish on the home or any other building on the property Satellite dishes are only to be installed on the ground. There will be a $100 nonrefundable charge to the resident's account if a satellite dish is installed on the roof.

THIS IS INTENDED TO BE A LEGALLY BINDING CONTRACT
If not fully understood, please seek the advice of an attorney before signing.

RESIDENT _____

DATE_____

RESIDENT _____

DATE_____

PROPERTY MANAGER_____
Roost Real Estate Co. AGENT

DATE_____

4

Lease Checklist
ROOST Real Estate Co.

Address _____

Tenant(s) _____

Approved Applicant / Before Signing

- ☐ Do we have the deposit?
- ☐ Do we have the pet deposit if applicable?
- ☐ Are we prorating the first month's rent?
- ☐ If so, how much do they need to bring to move in? _____
- ☐ Inform the applicant that we will ONLY accept a Money Order or Cashier's Check.
- ☐ Have applicant make arrangements to put utilities in their name(s) and provide confirmation numbers.
- ☐ Schedule date and time for lease signing.
- ☐ Remove lockbox and sign from property.
- ☐ Make copies of keys if needed.
- ☐ Place new tenant keys in their envelope.
- ☐ File office copy of key
- ☐ Prepare Lease Package for Tenant

At Lease Signing

- ☐ Have applicant sign/initial every section of lease and addendum package including deposit form.
- ☐ Collect deposit(s) and rent.
- ☐ Confirm all tenant information for Appfolio.
- ☐ Collect Gas and Electric service confirmation numbers:
    - o Ohio Edison_____
    - o Columbia Gas_____
- ☐ Complete Water Card if applicable.

After Lease Signing

- ☐ Scan and upload signed lease package to Appfolio.
- ☐ Mark property as 'Rented' and remove from marketing.
- ☐ Email owner confirmation and details.

Collecting Rent

Most of our tenants mail a check or money order to our office. Some pay in person as well. We do not accept cash for rent payments or security deposits. More and more of our tenants are choosing to pay their rent electronically through a personalized tenant portal we can create for them using Appfolio.

Our Management Fees

Our standard fees are outlined in our sample management agreement (See below). We charge a monthly fee based on a percentage of the rent collected. Our base fee is 10%, but we offer discounts to owners of large apartment complexes and large portfolios of scattered lot properties.

We charge a straight $200 for each new executed lease or lease renewal. We charge no additional leasing fees whatsoever. The $200 lease fee goes directly to the property manager and is the incentive portion of their overall compensation. It is important to me to stress that these are the only fees we charge. Unlike other management firms, we do not receive any kickbacks from vendors or mark-up services we contract for on our owners' behalf.

ROOST Real Estate Co.
PROPERTY MANAGEMENT AGREEMENT

THIS AGREEMENT is hereby entered into between _____ (Hereinafter "Owner" and ROOST Real Estate LLC. (Hereinafter "Agent"). Owner agrees to employ Agent as Owner's exclusive agent to rent, lease, operate and manage the real property located in the county of _____, State of _____ (hereinafter "Premises") for a period of one (1) year, commencing on _____ and ending on midnight _____.

The term hereof shall automatically renew for additional one (1) year periods on the same terms and conditions set forth herein, unless on or before sixty (60) days prior to the expiration of each said period, either party notifies the other in writing that it elects to change or terminate this Agreement; provided further, however, that either party may terminate this Agreement for good cause during the term hereof or any extension by giving to the other party not less than thirty (30) days prior written notice.

<u>Authority and Obligations of Agent</u>

1. To advertise the availability of the Premises for rent or for lease by placing signs on or near the Premises, advertising on the internet. To place a lock box on the Premises.

2. To negotiate, sign, renew or cancel rental agreements or lease option agreements, including leases, for the Premises. To negotiate leases for terms not to exceed <u>12 months</u> unless otherwise instructed by Owner.

3. To collect rents and security deposits or other charges and expenses due or to become due and to give receipts therefore. To deposit any receipts in the owner's bank accounts.

4. To serve such notices as are necessary and appropriate on tenants including, but not limited to, termination notices, notices to pay rent or quit and notices to comply with or quit. Rent is due on the 1st, late on the 5th and we post 3 Day Notices by the 10th.

5. To employ attorneys for the purpose of enforcing Owner's rights under rental agreements and leases and to institute and prosecute legal actions on behalf of Owner, to evict tenants to recover possession of the Premises and to recover rents and other sums due and settle, compromise and release such claims, actions or suits to reinstate such tenancies as Agent believes is appropriate for the benefit of Owner. Attorney fees to be paid by property owner.

6. To provide all services reasonably necessary for proper management of the Premises including periodic inspections, supervision of maintenance, arrangement for improvements, alterations, pest control repairs and decorations as may be required by Owner or deemed necessary by Agent for proper upkeep and rental of the Premises. Maintenance payroll if required in an occupied unit is billed at $29.00 per hour and in case of emergencies after business hours at $42.80 per hour. Mileage is charged between properties or to cover runs to obtain materials. Materials purchased on our accounts are billed at 110% of purchase price and tax to cover clerical and billing costs.

7. To purchase such supplies and enter into such contracts for repairs and maintenance of the Premises as may be necessary in the discretion of the Agent to provide proper upkeep for the Premises; provided, however, that Agent agrees not to expend in excess of $100.00 for any one item of repair; except for monthly or recurring operating charges and emergency repairs if, in the opinion of Agent, such repairs are necessary to protect the Premises from damage or to prevent to life or the property of other or to avoid suspension of necessary services or to avoid penalties or fines or to maintain services to tenants as may be called for in their rental agreements;

8. To hire, supervise and discharge all qualified, insured independent contractors required in the operation maintenance and upkeep of the property at rates of compensation to be determined and agreed upon by Owner and Agent when such total potential exceeds $100.00. Agent shall not be responsible for the misfeasance or malfeasance of said independent contractors if reasonable care has been exercised by the Agent in their appointment and retention;

9. To execute service contracts for electricity, gas, water cable, telephone, window cleaning, rubbish hauling and other services or utilities for the operation, maintenance and safety of the Premises as Agent and Owner may deem necessary; provided, however, that the items of such contract shall not exceed 12 months and the amount payable each month shall not exceed $100.00 without written approval of Owner;

10. To pay from receipts all operating expenses and such other expenses as may be authorized by Owner, including but not limited to, loan indebtedness, property taxes, special assessments and insurance premiums, and property management fees.

11. To maintain accurate and complete accounting records of all monies received and disbursed in connection with the management of the Premises which said records shall be opened for inspection by Owner during regular business hours and upon reasonable advance notice to Agent; provided, however, Agent shall submit on a monthly basis a written statement to Owner indicating cash receipts and disbursements during the previous month period.

<u>Obligation of Owner</u>

1. Indemnify and hold Agent harmless from any and all costs, expenses, attorney's fees, suits, liabilities, damages from or connected with the management of the Premises by Agent or the performance or exercise of any of the duties, obligations, powers and authorities herein or hereinafter granted to the Agent.

2. Not hold Agent liable for any error of judgment or for any mistake or fact or law, or for anything which Agent may do or refrain from doing hereinafter except where such act or omission is a result of willful misconduct or gross negligence.

3. Assume full responsibility for the payment of any expenses and obligations incurred in connection with the exercise of Agent's duties set forth in this Agreement.

4. Maintain adequate insurance coverage on all premises.

5. Accept full responsibility for any and all tenant deposits, in the event said deposits cannot be refunded from the operating account for the Premises while still maintaining an appropriate cash level in said operating account; Security Deposits shall remain in owner's operating account held by Agent.

6. Owner must notify Agent if they know of any lead-based paint or lead-based pant hazards at the Premises so that Agent can disclose any know information to Lessee(s) and provide to Lessee(s) any records available. Agent may sign on behalf of Owner all required disclosures and inform Lessee(s) of any known hazards or records pertaining to lead-paint and lead-paint hazards;

7. Deposit with Agent TBD as an initial operating reserve and will cover any excess of expenses over income within thirty (30) calendar days of any request by Agent. Failure to honor such request authorizes Agent to immediately terminate this Agreement.

8. Pay to Agent a management fee equal to 10% percent of all rent and other income from the Premises received or authorized to be received by the Agent, including any and all sums collected under any rental agreement.

9. Pay to Agent a Technical Service fee of $TBD per unit per month.

10. In addition to the foregoing management fee, pay to the Agent $TBD, upon execution of this Agreement, as a non-refundable setup fee for the purpose of creating an account for Owner and the various files and other mechanism used by the Agent in processing Agent's handling of Owner's business as referred to herein.

11. A check for the monthly management fee (10% of rent collected for the month) will be drawn on or before the 23rd of each month.

12. Pay to Agent for $200.00 for any new lease or renewal.

Assignment

This Agreement may not be assigned by Agent or Owner without the prior written consent of the other. In the event, however, such consent is granted and the Agreement is assigned, each of the covenants, conditions and obligations contained herein shall be binding upon and inure to the benefit of respective successors and assigns of Owner and Agent.

Severability

In the event any term or provisions of this Agreement shall be invalid or unenforceable, then the remainder of this Agreement shall not be affected thereby and each term and provision shall remain valid and enforceable to the fullest extent permitted.

Notification

All notices required to be given under this Agreement shall be in writing and mailed to the parties hereto at the addresses set forth below.

Attorney's Fees

In the event any legal action is required by either party to enforce the terms and provisions of the Agreement or arising out of the breach of any of the terms and provisions of this Agreement, the prevailing party shall be entitled to reasonable attorney's fees and court costs.

Entire Agreement

The foregoing contains the entire agreement of the parties and may not be changed, modified or altered except by a written document executed by Owner and Agent subsequent hereto.

By: _____ Dated: _____
     ROOST Real Estate LLC.

By: _____ Dated: _____
     Owner

Owner SS# or EIN#_____

ACCOUNTING

We use Appfolio for all of our accounting functions as well. Appfolio is an online cloud-based service that allows each of our owners to instantly access their reports and statements through an Owner Portal. Here is a summary of the Owner Portal from the www.Appfolio.com:

Hassle-Free Owner Portals

Owners need insight into the performance of their properties. As a property manager, do you have to print financial reports, copy invoices, and collate packets for your owners to send via snail mail? Do your owners get frustrated when they don't get paid on time? We've made the entire owner statement process more efficient with Appfolio's Owner Portal.

Instant Access To Reports

In addition to emailing Owner Statements every month, you can provide your owners with on-demand access to secure Owner Statements and reports. You can post current and historical Owner Statements to each Owner's Portal. You can also include any relevant reports so your owners can download these reports at their leisure. They will have access to the same Owner Statements you email on a monthly basis.

Personalize Owner Packets

You can pick and choose what information—invoices, work orders, financial statements—is consolidated and sent to each Owner with predetermined settings. You can choose whether to print or email the finished packet and how often to share it with your owner based on their specific requirements.

Quick And Direct Payment

You can cut your Owners a check directly through AppFolio software, or you can pay your Owners electronically, via direct deposit for faster and cheaper delivery.

Easy Password Recovery

The good news is that we've approached it in a unique way that won't result in Owners calling you when they forget their username and password (a common challenge with Owners Portals).

Source:
www.appfolio.com

Conclusion

We are always looking for new and innovative ways to streamline and improve our operations. Obviously the better we can serve our owners and tenant the more profitable our operation becomes. I am very proud of our team of professionals here at ROOST Real Estate Co. We have come a long way in a few short years, and we have even bigger plans for the future.

FUTURE OPPORTUNITIES

PART 8: FUTURE OPPORTUNITIES

I believe there are opportunities all over the country for real estate investors these days. As for me and my team, we will continue to invest and expand our business in Ohio in a big way. However, I am very excited about Florida these days. I see a big future in Florida for myself and for my investor clients. Specifically, we are focusing on Brevard County, also known as The Space Coast. We will be devoting a substantial amount of time and resources here over the next few years.

From the Melbourne Regional Chamber of Commerce Website:

Brevard County is located on the east coast of Central Florida just 35 miles east of Orlando, and home to such businesses as Harris, GE, NASA and the Kennedy Space Center, the only facility in the world that launched the Space Shuttle; Port Canaveral, the second-busiest cruise port in the world; 72 miles of beautiful Atlantic Ocean beaches; and the largest collection of endangered wildlife and plants in the continental United States. With its tropical weather, cultural activities, educational opportunities, active and passive recreation options, high-technology industries, and family-friendly atmosphere, the Space Coast offers an exceptional quality of life that residents and visitors enjoy year-round. With a small town feel and catering to the Florida lifestyle it's no wonder more than 500,000 people call its 16 municipalities and unincorporated areas "home."

http://www.everythingbrevard.com/Government/BrevardCountyInformation.html

ABOUT BREVARD COUNTY

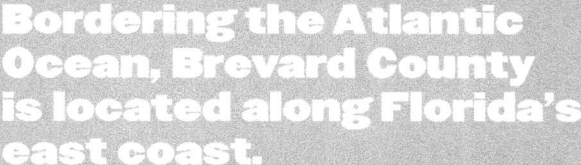

Bordering the Atlantic Ocean, Brevard County is located along Florida's east coast.

As of the 2010 census, the population was 543,376, making it the 10th largest county in Florida. The official county seat has been located in Titusville since 1894. Brevard County comprises the Palm Bay–Melbourne–Titusville, FL Metropolitan Statistical Area.

Influenced by the presence of the John F. Kennedy Space Center, Brevard County is also known as the **Space Coast**. As such, it was designated with the telephone area code 321, as in 3-2-1 liftoff. The county is named after Theodore Washington Brevard, an early settler, and state comptroller.

https://en.wikipedia.org/wiki/Brevard_County,_Florida

How we ended up here

Kelly and I had been visiting The Disney Vacation Club resort at Vero Beach at least annually since 2003. The resort is just south of Brevard county, about 30 miles from Melbourne Beach, Florida on A1A. We loved the area but never thought much about investing or working there.

Rena Smith, who has worked with us for almost 12 years relocated to West Melbourne, Florida in 2009. Rena helped us with our Springfield, Ohio REO division assisting with Broker Price Opinions from her home office both when she lived in Springfield and in Florida. We did not make the connection until 2014 that Rena and her husband Craig had relocated just north of Vero Beach. Craig transferred to the Space Coast area with PNC bank.

Once I took a closer look at the Melbourne area the more impressed I was. This area got hit hard during the recession but bounced back like very few other areas in the country have. Craig did extensive research on the area before agreeing to transfer with PNC. All in all, I know of no place in Florida I would rather be building a business. We seriously got to work when Rena earned her Florida Real Estate Sales Person license in early 2015.

TRENDS

 The median home value in Brevard County is $164,900.

Brevard County home values have gone up 10.6% over the past year.

 Zillow predicts they will rise 4.8% within the next year.

www.zillow.com/brevard-county-fl/home-values

The Melbourne Florida area is a great place for our current and future clients to expand their portfolio of rental properties. As of September 2016, we have 9 properties under management and expect to expand this business

CASE STUDIES OF PROPERTIES UNDER MANAGEMENT

At this time our owners are treating their investments as rental properties but an attractive alternative for many of our clients will be to sell these homes via land contract. Both the rental market and land contract markets are hot due to the number of people moving into the area. Many of these people are not yet in a position to obtain a mortgage and therefore welcome the option of a land contract.

For each of the case studies below I am showing both a rental scenario and a land contract scenario. I am using what I consider very conservative figures. You will see that insurance costs are estimated higher due to our proximity to the coast, but property taxes are in line, or even less than, what we see in Ohio.

The land contract exit strategy is a terrific option for many investors that could have a positive impact on their income tax liability. The land contract strategy also allows the investor to 'lock in' anticipated appreciation gains with a buyer now. For the buyer, at the end of the two or three year term, the final 'purchase' can be treated as a refinance which is often easier and quicker than a new purchase mortgage.

We have had great success marketing land contract purchases in Ohio for various clients by using all the marketing and screening tools we have developed over the years for our rental clients. Rently boxes, www.ROOSTRentals.com, Zillow, Facebook, and Appfolio have made the process of marketing, advertising, showing, and screening applications a routine process that just works. We have all of these tools in place in Florida right now.

Zillow.com has the last 12 months appreciation trend in the area at just under 11%. The home Kelly and I purchased in Melbourne last year has appreciated by almost 20% since November of 2015. I am using 6% in my case studies. I think that is an appropriately conservative approach.

GIBBS STREET, MELBOURNE FLORIDA

4 Bedrooms, 2 Baths
Purchase Price: $70,000.00

RENTAL ANALYSIS

PURCHASE PRICE:	$70,000.00
MONTHLY RENT:	$820.00
Annual Income:	$9,840.00
Vacancy Reserve:	-$492.00
Repair Reserve:	-$492.00
Insurance:	-$900.00
Property Taxes:	-$1,200.00
Mowing:	$0.00
Utilities:	$0.00
Pool Maintenance:	$0.00
Miscellaneous:	$0.00
Professional Management:	-$984.00
ANNUAL NET PROFIT:	$5,772.00
ROI:	8.25%
ESTIMATED APPRECIATION:	6%
ANNUAL ROI:	14.25

3 YEAR LAND CONTRACT SALE	
Sale Price:	$83,500.00(1)
Down Payment:	-$5,000.00
Land Contract Amount:	$78,500.00
Monthly Priciple and Interest:	$576.01(2)
Monthly Insurance:	$75.00
Property Taxes	$100.00
TOTAL PAYMENT:	$751.01
Annual Income:	$9,012.12
Vacancy Reserve:	$0.00
Repair Reserve:	$0.00
Insurance:	-$900.00
Property Taxes:	-$1,200.00
Mowing:	$0.00
Utilities:	$0.00
Pool Maintenance:	$0.00
Miscellaneous:	$0.00
Professional Management:	$0.00
ANNUAL NET PROFIT:	$6,912.12
ROI:	9.87%(3)
3 Years Annual Net Operating Profit:	$20,736.36
Downpayment:	$5,000.00
3% Commission on Land Contract Sale:	-$2,505.00
3% Remaining Commission at Cash Out:	-$2,505.00
Profit at Cash Out	$8,500.00(4)
Total Return after 3 years:	$29,226.36
Annualized Return	$9,742.12
ANNUAL ROI:	13.92%

(1) 19% Premium on $70,000
(2) 30 Amortizattion at 8%
(3) Annual Net Profit / Purchase Price
(4) Land Contract Amount less $70,000 Purchase Price

EDWARDS DRIVE, MELBOURNE FLORIDA

3 Bedrooms, 2 Baths
Purchase Price: $144,000.00

RENTAL ANALYSIS

PURCHASE PRICE:	$144,000.00
MONTHLY RENT:	$1,375.00
Annual Income:	$16,500.00
Vacancy Reserve:	-$825.00
Repair Reserve:	-$825.00
Insurance:	-$1,800.00
Property Taxes:	-$1,440.00
Mowing:	$0.00
Utilities:	$0.00
Pool Maintenance:	$0.00
Miscellaneous:	$0.00
Professional Management:	-$1,650.00
ANNUAL NET PROFIT:	$9,960.00
ROI:	6.92%
ESTIMATED APPRECIATION:	6%
ANNUAL ROI:	12.92

3 YEAR LAND CONTRACT SALE

Sale Price:	$170,000.00(1)
Down Payment:	-$5,000.00
Land Contract Amount	$165,000.00
Monthly Priciple and Interest:	$1,210.71(2)
Monthly Insurance:	$150.00
Property Taxes	$100.00
	$1,460.71
TOTAL PAYMENT:	
	$17,528.52
Annual Income:	
Vacancy Reserve:	$0.00
Repair Reserve:	$0.00
Insurance:	-$1,800.00
Property Taxes:	-$1,440.00
Mowing:	$0.00
Utilities:	$0.00
Pool Maintenance:	$0.00
Miscellaneous:	$0.00
Professional Management:	$0.00
ANNUAL NET PROFIT:	$14,288.52
ROI:	9.92%(3)
3 Years Annual Net Operating Profit:	$42,865.56
Downpayment:	$7,500.00
3% Commission on Land Contract Sale:	-$5,100.00
3% Remaining Commission at Cash Out:	-$5,100.00
Profit at Cash Out	$21,000.00(4)
Total Return after 3 years:	$61,165.56
Annualized Return	$20,388.52
ANNUAL ROI:	14.16%

(1) 19% Premium on $144,000
(2) 30 Amortizattion at 8%
(3) Annual Net Profit / Purchase Price
(4) Land Contract Amount less $144,000 Purchase Price

FAIRHAVEN, PALM BAY FLORIDA

3 Bedrooms, 2 Baths
Purchase Price: $120,000.00

RENTAL ANALYSIS

PURCHASE PRICE:	$120,000.00
MONTHLY RENT:	$1,170.00
Annual Income:	$14,040.00
Vacancy Reserve:	-$702.00
Repair Reserve:	-$702.00
Insurance:	-$900.00
Property Taxes:	-$1,332.00
Mowing:	$0.00
Utilities:	$0.00
Pool Maintenance:	$0.00
Miscellaneous:	$0.00
Professional Management:	-$1,404.00
ANNUAL NET PROFIT:	$9,000.00
ROI:	7.50%
ESTIMATED APPRECIATION:	6%
ANNUAL ROI:	13.5

3 YEAR LAND CONTRACT SALE

Sale Price:	$143,000.00 (1)
Down Payment:	-$5,000.00
Land Contract Amount	$138,000.00
Monthly Priciple and Interest:	$1,012.60 (2)
Monthly Insurance:	$150.00
Property Taxes	$111.00
TOTAL PAYMENT:	$1,273.60
Annual Income:	$15,283.20
Vacancy Reserve:	$0.00
Repair Reserve:	$0.00
Insurance:	-$900.00
Property Taxes:	-$1,332.00
Mowing:	$0.00
Utilities:	$0.00
Pool Maintenance:	$0.00
Miscellaneous:	$0.00
Professional Management:	$0.00
ANNUAL NET PROFIT:	$13,051.20
ROI:	10.88% (3)
3 Years Annual Net Operating Profit:	$39,153.60
Downpayment:	$5,000.00
3% Commission on Land Contract Sale:	-$4,290.00
3% Remaining Commission at Cash Out:	-$4,290.00
Profit at Cash Out	$18,000.00 (4)
Total Return after 3 years:	$53,573.60
Annualized Return	$17,857.87
ANNUAL ROI:	14.88%

(1) 19% Premium on $120,000
(2) 30 Amortizattion at 8%
(3) Annual Net Profit / Purchase Price
(4) Land Contract Amount less $120,000 Purchase Price

CHARLES DRIVE, PALM BAY FLORIDA

3 Bedrooms, 2 Baths, Pool Home
Purchase Price: $126,000.00

RENTAL ANALYSIS

PURCHASE PRICE:	$126,000.00
MONTHLY RENT:	$1,270.00
Annual Income:	$15,240.00
Vacancy Reserve:	-$762.00
Repair Reserve:	-$762.00
Insurance:	-$2,400.00
Property Taxes:	-$1,452.00
Mowing:	$0.00
Utilities:	$0.00
Pool Maintenance:	$0.00
Miscellaneous:	$0.00
Professional Management:	-$1,524.00
ANNUAL NET PROFIT:	$8,340.00
ROI:	6.62%
ESTIMATED APPRECIATION:	6%
ANNUAL ROI:	12.62

3 YEAR LAND CONTRACT SALE

Sale Price:	$150,000.00 (1)
Down Payment:	-$5,000.00
Land Contract Amount	$145,000.00
Monthly Priciple and Interest:	$1,063.96 (2)
Monthly Insurance:	$200.00
Property Taxes	$121.00
TOTAL PAYMENT:	$1,384.96
Annual Income:	$16,619.52
Vacancy Reserve:	$0.00
Repair Reserve:	$0.00
Insurance:	-$2,400.00
Property Taxes:	-$1,452.00
Mowing:	$0.00
Utilities:	$0.00
Pool Maintenance:	$0.00
Miscellaneous:	$0.00
Professional Management:	$0.00
ANNUAL NET PROFIT:	$12,767.52
ROI:	10.13% (3)
3 Years Annual Net Operating Profit:	$38,302.56
Downpayment:	$5,000.00
3% Commission on Land Contract Sale:	-$4,500.00
3% Remaining Commission at Cash Out:	-$4,500.00
Profit at Cash Out	$19,000.00 (4)
Total Return after 3 years:	$53,302.56
Annualized Return	$17,767.52
ANNUAL ROI:	14.10%

(1) 19% Premium on $126,000
(2) 30 Amortizattion at 8%
(3) Annual Net Profit / Purchase Price
(4) Land Contract Amount less $126,000 Purchase Price

COVENTRY CIRCLE, MELBOURNE FLORIDA

3 Bedrooms, 2 Baths, Fully Rehabbed
Purchase Price: $163,500.00

RENTAL ANALYSIS

PURCHASE PRICE:	$163,500.00
MONTHLY RENT:	$1,400.00
Annual Income:	$16,800.00
Vacancy Reserve:	-$840.00
Repair Reserve:	-$840.00
Insurance:	-$2,722.00
Property Taxes:	-$2,224.00
Mowing:	$0.00
Utilities:	$0.00
Pool Maintenance:	$0.00
Miscellaneous:	$0.00
Professional Management:	-$1,680.00
ANNUAL NET PROFIT:	$8,494.00
ROI:	5.20%
ESTIMATED APPRECIATION:	6%
ANNUAL ROI:	11.20

(1) 19% Premium on $163,500
(2) 30 Amortizattion at 8%
(3) Annual Net Profit / Purchase Price
(4) Land Contract Amount less $163,500 Purchase Price

3 YEAR LAND CONTRACT SALE	
Sale Price:	$198,500.00 (1)
Down Payment:	-$10,000.00
Land Contract Amount	$188,500.00
Monthly Priciple and Interest:	$1,254.10 (2)
Monthly Insurance:	$226.91
Property Taxes	$185.38
TOTAL PAYMENT:	$1,666.39
Annual Income:	$19,996.68
Vacancy Reserve:	$0.00
Repair Reserve:	$0.00
Insurance:	-$2,722.00
Property Taxes:	-$2,400.00
Mowing:	$0.00
Utilities:	$0.00
Pool Maintenance:	$0.00
Miscellaneous:	$0.00
Professional Management:	$0.00
ANNUAL NET PROFIT:	$14,874.68
ROI:	9.10% (3)
3 Years Annual Net Operating Profit:	$44,624.04
Downpayment:	$10,000.00
3% Commission on Land Contract Sale:	-$5,955.00
3% Remaining Commission at Cash Out:	-$5,955.00
Profit at Cash Out	$25,000.00 (4)
Total Return after 3 years:	$67,714.04
Annualized Return	$22,571.35
ANNUAL ROI:	13.81%

Full Disclosure: This one is a bit of a hypothetical. It is the house Kelly and I purchased in November of 2015. Like most homeowners, I think it is worth more than $198,500. We also use this house as our personal residence when we are in town and we have yet to find something that we like better. A good excercise nonetheless.

SHELBY DRIVE, MELBOURNE FLORIDA

3 Bedrooms, 1 Bath, Fully Rehabbed
Purchase Price: $99,900.00

RENTAL ANALYSIS

PURCHASE PRICE:	$99,900.00
MONTHLY RENT:	$925.00
Annual Income:	$11,100.00
Vacancy Reserve:	-$555.00
Repair Reserve:	-$555.00
Insurance:	-$900.00
Property Taxes:	-$1,020.00
Mowing:	$0.00
Utilities:	$0.00
Pool Maintenance:	$0.00
Miscellaneous:	$0.00
Professional Management:	-$1,110.00
ANNUAL NET PROFIT:	$6,960.00
ROI:	6.97%
ESTIMATED APPRECIATION:	6%
ANNUAL ROI:	12.97

3 YEAR LAND CONTRACT SALE	
Sale Price:	$119,000.00 (1)
Down Payment:	-$5,000.00
Land Contract Amount	$114,000.00
Monthly Priciple and Interest:	$836.49 (2)
Monthly Insurance:	$75.00
Property Taxes:	$85.00
TOTAL PAYMENT:	$996.49
Annual Income:	$11,957.88
Vacancy Reserve:	$0.00
Repair Reserve:	$0.00
Insurance:	-$900.00
Property Taxes:	-$1,020.00
Mowing:	$0.00
Utilities:	$0.00
Pool Maintenance:	$0.00
Miscellaneous:	$0.00
Professional Management:	$0.00
ANNUAL NET PROFIT:	$10,037.88
ROI:	10.05% (3)
3 Years Annual Net Operating Profit:	$30,113.64
Downpayment:	$5,000.00
3% Commission on Land Contract Sale:	-$3,570.00
3% Remaining Commission at Cash Out:	-$3,570.00
Profit at Cash Out	$14,100.00 (4)
Total Return after 3 years:	$42,073.64
Annualized Return	$14,024.55
ANNUAL ROI:	14.04%

(1) 19% Premium on $99,900
(2) 30 Amortizattion at 8%
(3) Annual Net Profit / Purchase Price
(4) Land Contract Amount less $99,900 Purchase Price

Vacation Property Management

We are also moving slowly into vacation property rentals. We are working with an owner of a home on Cocoa Beach that will rent weekly during peak seasons and monthly in the off seasons. Cocoa Beach is very interesting because of its proximity to Orlando and their theme parks. Cocoa Beach is aggressively marketing themselves as "Orlando's Beach." Once we work the kinks out of this new operation, we will begin expanding the service in mid to late 2017.

Final Installment of My Story

The Greater Fool Theory states that the price of an object is determined not by its intrinsic value, but rather by irrational beliefs and expectations of market participants. A price can be justified by a rational buyer under the belief that another party is willing to pay an even higher price.

Greater fool theory - Wikipedia, the free encyclopedia

https://en.wikipedia.org/wiki/Greater_fool_theory

During the crash and my long crawl from the wreckage I read John Kenneth Galbraith's 1955 book, The Great Crash 1929. I was looking for parallels to what we were living through in an attempt to make sense of it. It is a great book.

I had some experience in Florida during the boom. Myself, and several people I know attempted to do some 'pre-construction' deals in the Fort Myers area at the peak of the run up. The idea was to contract to have a home built at today's price and sell it to a new buyer at an inflated price prior to having to pay for the home. This was basically a play on the Greater Fool Theory. In almost all instances, my friends were left holding the bag when the music stopped.

I see no similarities with what we are seeing today in the Space Coast of Florida with what was happening in the early 2000's.

This economy is built on jobs—good jobs. The boom in the early 2000's was built on the availability of a lot of very cheap money. The Space Coast in my opinion has it all. It is a great place to work and raise a family.

Given where I am today I find it interesting that Florida was on my mind in early 2009. Smart investors made a lot of money in Florida after the crash—just as I predicted they would. I really believe my clients and I have a good chance to do the same over the next few years.

FLORIDA—BOOM AND BUST
JANUARY 2009

Consider this description of a speculative real estate bubble:

...Miami, Miami Beach, Coral Gables, the East Coast as far north as Palm Beach, and the cities over on the Gulf had been struck by the great Florida real estate boom. The Florida boom contained all the elements of the classic speculative bubble. There was the indispensable element of substance. Florida had a better winter climate than New York, Chicago, or Minneapolis. Higher incomes and better transportation were making it increasingly accessible to the frost-bound North. The time indeed was coming when the annual flight to the South would be as regular and impressive as the migrations of the Canada goose.

Now consider this description of a speculative bubble bursting by the same author:

...On that indispensable element of fact men and women had proceeded to build a world of speculative make-believe. This is a world inhabited not by people who have to be persuaded to believe but by people who want an excuse to believe. In the case of Florida, they wanted to believe that the whole peninsula would soon be populated by the holiday-makers and the sun worshippers of a new and remarkably indolent era. So great would be the crush that beaches, bogs, swamps, and common scrubland would all have value. The Florida climate did not ensure that this would happen. But it did enable people who wanted to believe it would happen so to believe.

Sounds like this was written recently doesn't it? It wasn't. These words are those of the famous economist John Kenneth Galbraith from his 1955 classic work, The Great Crash of 1929. The Great Crash 1929 describes in detail the events that led up to the stock market crash of 1929, the aftermath, and his interpretation of cause and consequence.

Galbraith opens his book with an account of the Florida real estate boom and bust of the 1920's.

Anyone who reads Galbraith's words and is the least bit familiar with the recent Florida real estate market will be struck dumb by the eerie similarities between the market of 80 years ago and today.

We have been through this before! How could we not be conscious of these facts? Did we really think all of those old jokes about Florida swampland to sell had no basis in reality? The story of the Florida real estate boom and bust is a classic example of the adage; those of us ignorant of the past are doomed to repeat it.

As someone familiar with much of the pre-construction, get-rich-quick, 'investment' opportunities so prevalent in south Florida during the middle of this decade, I can say without a doubt, we wanted to believe. We bet that the Florida climate and booming economy would continue to attract people to the area, and it probably will, but not in time to save people who find themselves holding property worth a fraction of the money owed. There were more Realtor's, mortgage brokers, builders and speculative investors than the swelling population could support.

I visited the Naples and Fort Myers areas at the peak of the bubble in late 2005. We saw new homes, schools, roads, and strip centers being built everywhere. However, I also saw huge tracts of land subdivided and laid out for new homes, streets already in place, with no activity whatsoever. Even in the midst of the frenzy, it seemed like it would take years for these lots to be absorbed by the swelling population. But I too wanted to believe.

I encourage every investor looking to make sense of today's economic reality to read The Great Crash 1929. It is a relatively quick book, and surprisingly entertaining given the subject matter. Galbraith will shape how you evaluate future investment opportunities of all types, not just real estate opportunities.

As with any bust, there are opportunities for knowledgeable and savvy investors to make money. Florida real estate is no different. No one can say for certain that the market has hit bottom yet, but someone investing for cash flow with a seven to ten year time horizon, will find opportunity. At My Real Estate Life, we believe in basic fundamentals. Buy low, cash flow, hold the property for appreciation. We, of course, hope appreciation occurs sooner rather than later.

We want to hear your thoughts on this post and any other aspects of real estate investing. Join us today at www.MyRealEstateLIfeOnline.com.

ABOUT THE AUTHOR

Chris McAllister was born and raised in Springfield, Ohio and graduated from The Ohio State University with a degree in Communication in 1982. He also earned a Master of Arts in Organizational Management (MAOM) in the late 1990's.

Chris worked in single and multi-unit retail management throughout the Midwest and Northeastern United States from 1985 through 2000. His last assignment was opening and managing Target stores on Long Island and in Queens NYC.

Chris returned home to Ohio in late 2000. He entered the real estate business as a licensed sales agent in Ohio in 2001. He earned his broker license in Ohio in 2003 and became a licensed broker in Florida in 2013. He was a RE/MAX franchisee from 2003 to 2009 and was affiliated with Real Estate II, a well- established local brokerage from May 2009 until December 2013. He earned his real estate broker license in Florida in 2014.

Chris has also invested in rental properties over the last decade and co-wrote the book, We Lost $1,000,0000 in Real Estate in Less than Five Years – And You Can Too!. The book, released in 2009, details the ups and downs Chris and his partners experienced in hopes that their readers avoid making the same mistakes they did.

Chris and the McAllister Team were recognized by the Ohio Association of Realtors as a Top 5 award winner for transaction sides closed in 2010, 2011, 2012, and 2013. In addition, The McAllister Team manages hundreds of individual housing units within a 50 mile radius of downtown Springfield.

Chris's unique ability is creating business opportunities and strategies designed to support and add value to the lives of real estate professionals and their clients. Chris created ROOST Real Estate Co. as his platform for helping people get the most out of their real estate investments whether they are investors, owner occupants, or tenants.

ROOST Real Estate Co. is located in The Bushnell Building in Springfield, Ohio. ROOST was conceived in 2013 by Chris McAllister, a real estate broker and investor. New Ohio Real Estate LLC DBA Roost Real Estate Co. is a licensed real estate brokerage in Ohio. ROOST Real Estate LLC DBA ROOST Real Estate Co. is a licensed real estate broker in Florida. Real Estate Brands Ltd is the future franchising entity for ROOST Real Estate Co. and Lucky Town Real Estate Co.

Chris@ROOSTRealEstateCo.com / 844.806.6577

www.ROOSTRealEstateCo.com

www.facebook.com/ROOSTRealEstateCo

A DIFFERENT KIND OF BROKERAGE

We are not your typical broker. That's a great thing!

Most brokerages have two lines of business. They work with buyers and they work with sellers. At Real Estate Brands Ltd, we work with buyers and sellers too, but we also work with investors, and the people who rent from them.

Embracing 100% of all of the people who need a home, not just the 60% to 65% of the people who own real estate, creates a very different kind of Real Estate Company for our clients and for our agents.

We work closely with investors. We help investors find, evaluate, purchase, and manage investment property. By offering Property Management services to our investors, they are more comfortable buying more property.

Some people who rent their homes do so for their entire lives. Others will only rent for a few years before buying a home of their own. We help our tenant clients become home owners.

Because we work in the property management business, we have relationships with skilled trade's people that can help all of our listing clients prepare and maintain their properties for sale.

The Real Estate Brands Ltd family of companies are all referral based businesses. We believe that the very best clients are those that are recommended by our existing and past clients. We have a referral based marketing system that keeps all of our brands top of mind with everyone we work with.

Our tenants become buyers, and refer new tenants and new buyers to us. Our investors become repeat buyers, referring new investors and new buyers, and new sellers to us. Our buyers and sellers refer their friends, family and co-workers again and again.

We are the real estate company people turn to at every stage of their lives. We are there when our clients rent their first apartment, buy their first home, buy their first investment property, and buy their retirement villa on the beach.

REAL ESTATE BRANDS LTD.
Smart. Passionate. Supportive. Approachable.

Meeting people where they are today, and helping them get to where they want to be tomorrow.

APPENDIX

APPENDIX - BUSINESS PLAN OUTLINE

This is the business plan outline I use to communicate with my bank. Feel free to adapt it to your needs as you see fit.

New Ohio Investments LLC

A real estate investment company focused on profitably providing affordable housing in Springfield, Ohio.

Business Plan, July 2014

Chris McAllister
14 East Main Street
Suite 120
Springfield, Ohio 45502

Table of Contents

I About New Ohio Investments LLC

II Current Rent Roll

III Loan Summary

IV Annual Return on Investment by Property 2013

V Projected Return on Investment by Property 2014

VI Key Projects and Requested Line of Credit

VII Future Investments

VIII Financial Reports
- Balance Sheet
- 2013 Profit and Loss Statement
- YTD 2014 Profit and Loss Statement

▎About New Ohio Investments LLC

Chris McAllister formed New Ohio Investments LLC in 2009 as a real estate investment company focused on purchasing inexpensive properties and rehabbing them over time from cash flow. The strategy was to secure enough property so that the resulting cash flow would be equal to $7000 per month once the initial land contract financing was paid off and the properties were all placed in service.

New Ohio Real Estate LLC DBA ROOST Real Estate Co. manages the properties—an entity owned by Chris McAllister. ROOST Real Estate Co. manages approximately 600 rental properties for 70+ individual owners. ROOST Real Estate Co. manages and will continue to manage New Ohio Investments LLC properties at cost.

Managing these types of properties is very labor intensive, however, returns on investment can approach 25%+ in any given year and management expects average returns after all expenses to average 15% to 20%. As a rule the company forecasts vacancy rates of 10% to 20% and repairs and maintenance at 20% to 25%

II Current Rent Roll

ADDRESS	RENT
Light Unit 1	$295
Light Unit 2	$295
Light Unit 2	$295
Light Unit 2	$295
W High up	$375
W High down	$265
Cleveland	$395
W Washington	$525
Belmont	$450
Oak	$550
S Limestone	$300
S Limestone	$450
Kenton	$600
East Liberty	$495
E Southern	$595
Fountain	$350
Fountain	$300
Fountain	$325
Fountain	$275
Fountain	$195
Columbus	$565
Edwards	$575
S Limestone	$595
Keifer	$520
Shaffer	$495
Isabella	$495
Sherman	$425
Sherman	$425
Pleasant	$0
E Johnson	$0
Limestone	$0
S Wittenberg	$0
E Rose	$0
Center	$0
Center	$0
Highland	$0
Berger	$0
	$11,720

III Loan Summary

The table below details the purchase price, date purchased, original loan amount, current balance and date loan will be paid off.

IV Annual Return on Investment by Property 2013

Address	2013 Operating Profit	WIP Purchase Price	Upgrades	Total	ROI
Light	-$5,479	$8,100	$16,014	$24,114	-22.72%
W High	-$7,435	$5,500	$9,666	$15,166	-49.02%
Cleveland	$593	$5,500	$9,188	$14,688	4.04%
W Washington	$5,349	$4,000	$17,685	$21,685	24.67%
Belmont	$3,516	$11,000	$6,751	$17,751	19.81%
Oak	$4,463	$7,000	$11,704	$18,704	23.86%
S Limestone	$4,495	$11,000	$14,625	$25,625	17.54%
Kenton	$644	$7,777	$25,266	$33,043	1.95%
E Liberty	-$6,965	$2,500	$13,801	$16,301	-42.73%
E Southern	$3,623	$10,000	$6,713	$16,713	21.68%
Fountain	-$4,228	$11,000	$5,896	$16,896	-25.02%
Columbus	-$3,465	$12,000	$4,538	$16,538	-20.95%
Edwards	$4,926	$11,000	$10,289	$21,289	23.14%
S Limestone	$0	$15,000	$0	$15,000	0.00%
Keifer	$0	$7,000	$8,868.00	$15,868.00	0.00%
Isabella	$0	$5,000	$8,307.00	$13,307.00	0.00%
Sherman	$0	$3,000	$11,000.00	$14,000.00	0.00%
N Shafer	$0	$15,000	$0.00	$15,000.00	0.00%
W Pleasant	$0	$5,000	$0.00	$5,000.00	0.00%
E Johnson	$0	$4,000	$0.00	$4,000.00	0.00%
S Limestone	$0	$8,800	$0.00	$8,800.00	0.00%
S Wittenberg	$0	$2,000	$0.00	$2,000.00	0.00%
E Rose	$0	$2,000	$0.00	$2,000.00	0.00%
Center	$0	$20,000	$0.00	$20,000.00	0.00%
Highland	$0	$2,000	$0.00	$2,000.00	0.00%
Berger	$0	$2,000	$0.00	$2,000.00	0.00%
	$37	$197,177	$180,311	$377,488.00	0.01%

A Real Estate Investor's Guide to Profitability

V Projected Return on Investment by Property 2014

Address	Through July 31 Operating Profit	Projected Full Year	WIP Purchase Price	Upgrades	Total	ROI
Light	$2,386	$4,090.29	$8,100	$16,014	$24,114	16.96%
W High	$2,487	$4,263.43	$5,500	$9,666	$15,166	28.11%
Cleveland	$1,916	$3,284.57	$5,500	$9,188	$14,688	22.36%
W Washington	$2,156	$3,696.00	$4,000	$17,685	$21,685	17.04%
Belmont	$2,003	$3,433.71	$11,000	$6,751	$17,751	19.34%
Oak	$3,111	$5,333.14	$7,000	$11,704	$18,704	28.51%
S Limestone	$3,189	$5,466.86	$11,000	$14,625	$25,625	21.33%
Kenton	$3,151	$5,401.71	$7,777	$25,266	$33,043	16.35%
E Liberty	$2,563	$4,393.71	$2,500	$13,801	$16,301	26.95%
E Southern	-$2,572	$1,250.00	$10,000	$6,713	$16,713	7.48%
Fountain	$4,116	$7,056.00	$11,000	$5,896	$16,896	41.76%
Columbus	$891	$1,527.43	$12,000	$4,538	$16,538	9.24%
Edwards	-$1,140	$1,250.00	$11,000	$10,289	$21,289	5.87%
S Limestone	-$956	$1,000.00	$15,000	$0	$15,000	6.67%
Keifer	-$2,305	$1,000.00	$7,000	$8,868.00	$15,868.00	6.30%
Isabella	$0	$0.00	$5,000	$8,307.00	$13,307.00	0.00%
Sherman	$0	$0.00	$3,000	$11,000.00	$14,000.00	0.00%
N Shafer	$0	$1,000.00	$15,000	$0.00	$15,000.00	6.67%
W Pleasant	$0	$0.00	$5,000	$0.00	$5,000.00	0.00%
E Johnson	$0	$0.00	$4,000	$0.00	$4,000.00	0.00%
S Limestone	$0	$0.00	$8,800	$0.00	$8,800.00	0.00%
S Wittenberg	$0	$0.00	$2,000	$0.00	$2,000.00	0.00%
E Rose	$0	$0.00	$2,000	$0.00	$2,000.00	0.00%
Center	$0	$0.00	$20,000	$0.00	$20,000.00	0.00%
Highland	$0	$0.00	$2,000	$0.00	$2,000.00	0.00%
Berger	$0	$0.00	$2,000	$0.00	$2,000.00	0.00%
	$20,996	$53,446.86	$197,177	$180,311	$377,488	14.16%

VI Key Projects and Requested Line of Credit

New Ohio Investments LLC is seeking a $40,000 line of credit to finance specific real estate projects detailed below. New Ohio Investments LLC will seek to pay down the line of credit with financing to term on Center, South Limestone, and eventually South Fountain Ave. (The South Fountain Avenue property is in the Historic District and ripe for rehab in the next one to three years.) Permanent financing will be no more than 50% loan to value over a 10 year term.

CONDITION / FINANCE PLAN

Address	Need	Who	How	Est.	When	
Line of Credit and Refinance						
Center	Full Interior	WesBanco	Loc / Refi	$40,000	Now	
Limestone	Full interior.	WesBanco	Loc / Refi	$20,000	Next	
Pleasant	Full Rehab		Cash flow	$20,000	In this order.	Dec-14
E Johnson	Full Rehab		Cash flow	$20,000	In this order.	Apr-15
S Wittenberg	Full Rehab		Cash flow	$20,000	In this order.	Aug-15
E Rose	Full Rehab		Cash flow	$20,000	In this order.	Dec-15
Highland	Full Rehab		Cash flow	$20,000	In this order.	Apr-16
Berger	Full Rehab		Cash flow	$20,000	In this order.	Aug-16
Want to do Project						
Fountain	Roof / Exterior Paint	WesBanco	Loc / Refi	$30,000	2016	South Fountain Historic District
Upgrades to do over time.						
Oak	Siding		Cash flow	$8,000	2015	Next Tenant
S Limestone	Exterior Paint		Cash flow	$5,000	2015	Next Tenant
Light	Roof, Porches		Cash flow	$16,000	2016	As Needed
Kenton	Will need roof		Cash flow	$8,000	2017	As Needed
Shafer	Interior paint/ Exterior paint		Cash flow	$5,000	2015	Next Tenant

Properties Complete w/ Equity Available as Collateral			Market Value	50%
Limestone	None	Available Equity as Collateral	$30,000.00	$15,000.00
E Liberty	None	Available Equity as Collateral	$24,000.00	$12,000.00
E Southern	None	Available Equity as Collateral	$22,500.00	$11,250.00
Columbus	None	Available Equity as Collateral	$22,000.00	$11,000.00
Edwards	None	Available Equity as Collateral	$27,500.00	$13,750.00
Isabella	None	Available Equity as Collateral	$16,000.00	$8,000.00
Sherman	None	Available Equity as Collateral	$22,000.00	$11,000.00
			$164,000.00	$67,000.00
Complete W/ Loans in Place				
W High	None	encumbered		
Cleveland	None	encumbered		
W Washington	None	encumbered		

VII Future Investments

The company has no plans at this time to purchase additional properties within the Springfield city limits. NOI's plan is to put all currently inventoried properties in service before purchasing more properties. However, the company will consider opportunities to diversify the portfolio with higher end properties outside of the city limits should they arise.

VIII Financial Reports

Please see attached:

- Balance Sheet as of July 31, 2014
- Balance Sheet as of December 31, 2013
- 2013 Profit and Loss Statement
- YTD 2014 Profit and Loss Statement

www.ingramcontent.com/pod-product-compliance
Lightning Source LLC
Chambersburg PA
CBHW070027210526
45170CB00012B/211